MODERN PSALMS

Volume One
In The Beginning

MODERN PSALMS

Volume One
In The Beginning

Modern Psalms, Volume 1: In the Beginning
Copyright © 2025 by PCM
First Paperback Edition: December 2025

All rights reserved. No part of this publication may be reproduced, stored in a retrieval system, or transmitted in any form or by any means – electronic, mechanical, photocopy, recording, or otherwise – without the prior written consent of the author. The only exception is brief quotations in printed reviews.

Unless otherwise indicated, all Scripture quotations are taken from The Holy Bible, NEW INTERNATIONAL VERSION® NIV® Copyright © 1973, 1978, 1984, 2011 by Biblica, Inc. Used with permission. All rights reserved worldwide. Scripture quotations marked ESV are from the ESV® Bible (The Holy Bible, ENGLISH STANDARD VERSION®), © 2001 by Crossway, a publishing ministry of Good News Publishers. Text Edition: 2016. Used by permission. All rights reserved. Scripture quotations marked KJV are taken from the King James Version. Public Domain.

To order products, or for any other correspondence, contact:

KINGDOM BRIDGES
PUBLISHING

Kingdom Bridges Publishing
78 Folly Rd. Blvd. B9–1135
Charleston, SC 29407
www.kingdombn.com
Tel.: 843-732-9377
E-mail: admin@kingdombn.com
Or reach us on Facebook & Instagram: @kingdombridgespublishing

Chief Editor: Julie A. Weigel
Interior images: PCM, created with AI assistance
Book cover design: Kingdom Bridges Publishing

ISBN: 979-8-9932193-3-2

Printed in the United States of America.

TABLE OF CONTENTS

Foreword vii
Introduction ix
Statement of Faith xi
How to Use This Devotional xiii

I No Longer Live 1
Forever Changed 9
Childlike Faith 21
Son of No One 31
Church Hurt 43
Unbreakable Love 51
Life We Built Together 61
Follow Me 69
God Moment 75
Love of a Father 85
Witness the Spirit 97
Take Me as I Am 105
Perfect Timing 113
In My Darkest Hour 121
My Feet Are Planted 133

About the Author 145
About Piero DiGilio 147

Foreword

IF YOU ARE LOOKING FOR an in-depth dive into the heart behind the worship-filled lyrics of a Christian hip-hop artist, you will find great joy as you turn the pages of this book and begin to understand the foundation of Scripture that surrounds and fuels the spirit of the music now put to paper.

PCM has become a friend of mine over the past couple of years, and I can say that I have stood beside him on a stage as he guided the hearts of men toward discipleship beyond the pews of a building. I am honored to share my thoughts on this incredibly well-written book, which takes you on a journey through his first fifteen songs—showing how they connect to the Bible and how they apply to your own walk with Christ. Whether you are a teenager just beginning to understand the love of Jesus or a seasoned elder with a strong foundation of faith, this book will sharpen your weapons of warfare.

We have been called to run a race until the end, when we stand before God on that beautiful day our hearts long for. I would even say that reading is a way of running in the Spirit. What's incredible about this book is that it transcends musical genres. The beat is stripped down, the voice of humanity is removed, and all that remains is Bible-based encouragement that sings songs of praise from the pages straight to your heart. My hope is that each song will deepen your understanding of the author's heart, and that each sentence will help root you more firmly in the art of praise, honor, and glory that God bestows upon His followers.

Have you ever read the Song of Solomon? There is something deeply intimate about the flow of musical poetry describing love for the one who is cherished. In the same way, each page of this book tells a story of brokenness, hope, pain, redemption, and truth. At times, I hear a worship song on the radio and wish I could understand the testimony behind it—why it was written, what level of joy or pain inspired it, and how the artist made it through that season of life. That is exactly what this book does: it answers those questions.

Maybe you've never listened to Christian hip-hop—or Christian music at all. The author's heart is to introduce you to the anointing that flows from God to you, and back to God, through praise, obedience, trials, and life itself. Each song points you to the foundation of truth and shows how that truth can break down barriers that may have held you back for far too long. Take each page and each song and walk through them patiently as you begin to understand God, music, and the heart of my good friend, PCM.

Blessings to you as you allow the melody of the music to speak to you.

— Blake Martin

Introduction

MY NAME IS PCM. I'M A Christian Music Artist, and a first-time author. As a devout follower of Christ, I don't adhere to any specific denomination, instead striving to live by the teachings of Jesus and the Apostles, guided by the Holy Bible.

For those unfamiliar with my music, you may not know that I wear a mask and keep my identity private. I do this so the masked image can represent anyone who is currently in pursuit of a relationship with Jesus Christ, making it more relatable to those on a similar journey.

I've been a believer in Christ my whole life, but it wasn't until 2018 that I truly developed a personal relationship with Him. In 2023, while praying, a chorus began to echo in my mind: "It's no longer I that live, but Christ that lives in me." No matter how hard I tried, I couldn't shake those words. I became convinced that God was leading me in a new direction. That chorus became the foundation of my song "I No Longer Live," marking the beginning of my musical ministry.

I pray—and truly believe—that through this music ministry, seeds of faith will be planted that not only produce hope, but also help pave the way toward establishing a ministry that offers housing and employment to those who are lost, helping them rebuild their lives with Christ as their guiding light.

Modern Psalms, Volume 1, In the Beginning, captures the first fifteen songs of a raw and formative journey in which I sought to find my voice. As you move into newer releases with a more polished sound, I pray you will still appreciate the authenticity of melodies born from discovering the gift God placed within me.

This book follows those first songs—early steps that helped shape both my musical direction and my faith. While they may not reflect my current musical level, they are the foundation that led me here and strengthened my walk with Christ. Each song marks a moment along my spiritual path. Within these pages, I share the Scriptures that inspired them, the thoughts and experiences behind their creation, and what they mean to me personally.

I pray and believe that through this ministry—both in music and in message—God will use these songs to plant seeds of faith.

> *"Let the message of Christ dwell among you richly*
> *as you teach and admonish one another with all wisdom*
> *through psalms, hymns, and songs from the Spirit,*
> *singing to God with gratitude in your hearts."*
> —Colossians 3:16

Statement of Faith

I believe in the Triune God—Father, Son, and Holy Spirit. God the Father is the Creator of heaven and earth, sovereign, loving, but just, who desires a relationship with His creation. He governs all things with justice, mercy, and compassion.

Jesus Christ, the Son of God, is my Savior and Lord. He was sent by the Father to live a sinless life, die on the cross for our sins, and rise again, defeating death and offering salvation to all who believe in Him. My relationship with Jesus is deeply personal—one that I have spent years cultivating. It is only by His divine mercy that I am granted salvation, and I give Him all the glory for it.

The Holy Spirit lives within me as well as all believers—guiding, comforting, and empowering us to live in accordance with God's will. He helps us pray and will pray on our behalf. He produces the fruit of our salvation, leading us into good works as an expression of our faith and transformation in Christ.

I believe that salvation is a gift of grace, received through faith in Jesus Christ, not earned by our works. However, true faith is never without evidence. The fruit of our salvation naturally leads us to do good works, not to earn favor, but as a response to the love and grace we have received.

I am not a Bible scholar, and I encourage everyone to read the Bible for themselves and seek God's truth directly through His Word. As I have grown in my walk with Christ, I've adopted the belief that while human understanding may falter, God's Word remains true.

"Let God be true, and every man a liar."
—Romans 3:4

How to Use This Devotional

Modern Psalms is a unique devotional experience designed to be both read and heard. Each chapter includes original song lyrics, guiding you to reflect on God's presence and power, and to deepen your understanding of His Word.

Each devotional is structured as follows:

❖ Song Lyrics

Each chapter begins with original lyrics written as modern-day psalms. These words are meant to be read slowly and prayerfully, allowing them to speak directly to your heart. At the top of each lyric page, you'll find a QR code—scan it with your smartphone or tablet to listen to the corresponding song on YouTube. Experiencing the music while reading brings the lyrics to life, enhancing your time of reflection and worship.

❖ The Message Behind the Song

This section offers insight into the heart, testimony, and inspiration behind each song. It explains what the author experienced, how God revealed His truth, and the spiritual lessons woven into the lyrics.

❖ Biblical Study

Each entry concludes with a focused study of Scripture. These passages connect the lyrics to God's Word and invite you to reflect more deeply on the truth of the Gospel, the character of Christ, and God's plan for your life.

There is no right or wrong way to move through this devotional. You may read it in any order and use it in many ways—daily, weekly, during times of worship, or whenever you need encouragement. Let the Holy Spirit guide your journey through the words, music, and Scripture, allowing them to draw you closer to Christ.

May this devotional strengthen your faith, quiet your mind, and remind you that His voice is always within reach.

"Sing to the Lord a new song;
sing to the Lord, all the earth."
— Psalm 96:1

I No Longer Live

(Jesus)

[Chorus]
It's no longer I that live, it's Christ that lives within me
It's no longer I that live, it's Christ that lives within me (Jesus)
I died that day on the cross with Him, it's He who pays my wage of sin
It's no longer I that live, it's Christ that lives within me (Jesus)
It's no longer I that live, it's Christ that lives within me
My flesh was filled with worldly sins, yet He still forgives me (Jesus)
I died that day on the cross with Him, it's He who pays my wage of sin
It's no longer I that live, it's Christ that lives within me (Jesus)

This world hurts, but Jesus saves,
I'm trying to prepare you for the last days
Wanna make sure that your faith isn't just a phase
If you're saved by His grace, you'll never see the grave
Give up all your pain, give up all your shame
Church is when two people say and worship His name
You got nothing to lose and everything to gain
You may be broken inside, but He's known to heal the lame
I was living in death, but He gave me life
Learned to walk in faith and not by sight
His return will be like a thief in the night
But I died in darkness, now I live in the light

[Chorus]

Give yourself to death, give yourself to death
Let your soul be reborn in His holiness
This world is a mess, we're overburdened and stressed
Jesus said, follow Me and I'll lead you to rest

There's nothing to fear, the Holy Spirit is near
I don't want your tears, but brother lend me your ears
Open up your soul, let Him make you whole
Jesus, Jesus, come and take me home

Amazing grace, trumps selfish pride
and His righteousness it shines so bright
I was a thief on the cross, dying by His side
And Jesus said, come to paradise

[Chorus]

Behind the Song

THIS IS THE SONG THAT STARTED it all! At the time, I had been praying for a way to begin a ministry that would offer housing and support for former convicts. I remember being in the shower when the lyrics for "I No Longer Live" suddenly came to me. It was stuck in my mind, and no matter what I did, it was indelible. I knew this was something given to me by God, but I wasn't sure what to do with it; I had no ambition or creative drive to make music, let alone Christian music.

After a few weeks of trying to ignore the nudging, I finally submitted to it and decided to try writing a song. The moment I sat down to write, I was amazed at how easily the words flowed from my pen. Line after line came to me as if someone were speaking through me. In less than an hour, the song was complete. But then I thought, "What next?" I had the lyrics, but no melody or music to go with it.

I began searching the internet for instrumentals, but I quickly realized how expensive exclusive rights were—most were priced around $1,000, which was far beyond my reach. I continued searching, trying to find something that fit both the lyrics and the vision in my head. It was at that point that I came across a beat produced by Piero Digilio. It was perfect. I knew I had to have it, but I also knew my financial situation didn't agree. So, I reached out to Piero.

I explained to him that I was writing a Christian song and that I believed the inspiration was divine. After several exchanges, he resonated with the message. He, too, felt that secular music had become too satanic. In a show of generosity, he offered me a great deal on the instrumental track. Little did I know that this interaction would not only give life to the song but would also mark the beginning of a lifelong friendship with someone I now consider my brother in Christ.

With everything in place, I found a local studio to record the song. However, during the process, I quickly discovered that I couldn't sing, and the chorus needed a powerful voice to bring it to life. I reached out to various Christian groups, looking for someone who could deliver the chorus with the care and passion it deserved. Within minutes, Rob Ruff contacted me. I sent him what I had recorded and explained my vision for the chorus. Rob gave me some excellent advice on music equipment and then agreed to sing it.

I waited several days, anxiously anticipating what he would create. I checked in periodically for updates and soon realized that Rob was a perfectionist. When he finally sent me the recording, I stared at the email, nervous to hit "play." Mustering the courage, I listened to it—and was blown away. His voice was stunning, like nothing I had ever heard before. The song was now complete.

Upon hearing the finished product, I knew deep down that this was something I needed to continue. During the writing process of "I No Longer Live," the only thing on my mind was trusting God. I wanted the song to reflect the seriousness and sincerity of Apostle Paul when he wrote in Galatians 2:20, *"I have been crucified with Christ and I no longer live, but Christ lives in me. The life I now live in the body, I live by faith in the Son of God, who loved me and gave himself for me."*

The power of that verse amazes me. The idea that someone can completely die to their old identity—their heritage, their past, all the good and bad that once defined them—and embrace a new identity in Christ is astounding. This is what we are called to do as believers. We must learn to completely surrender ourselves to Jesus if we truly want to experience salvation.

I know it's a daunting and scary thought. From a young age, we're taught to be independent, to take control of our own lives, and to rely on ourselves. As children, we are often told to sit down, be quiet, and not make a scene. But in Christ, we are called to do the opposite. He wants us to rejoice loudly, proclaim the Good News to the ends of the earth, and live boldly in faith.

I understand that for some—especially those who have a fear of public speaking or engagement—that this may seem terrifying. But we must look beyond our fears and let the Holy Spirit take control. In Mark 13:11, Jesus reassures us, *"Whenever you are arrested and brought to trial, do not worry beforehand about what to say. Just say whatever is given you at the time, for it is not you speaking, but the Holy Spirit."* We don't have to rely on our own abilities or words—the Holy Spirit will guide us in those crucial moments.

There's a line in the song that says, "I want to make sure your faith isn't just a phase." This is a direct reference to the parable of the Sower that Jesus taught in Matthew 13:1–23. In this parable, many seeds are scattered, but only a few takes root and grow. This is a vivid illustration of how many people hear the Gospel but not all truly receive it in their hearts.

I want to be a part of helping those seeds of faith grow—especially the ones that fall on the wayside, rocky ground, and among the thorns. These are the people who might hear the Word but face obstacles, distractions, or challenges that prevent their faith from growing deep roots. My hope is that I might encourage and support them so their faith can grow strong, endure, and bear fruit.

Belief in Christ transforms our entire existence. When we place our faith in Him, we don't just adopt a new way of living, we become eternal beings, destined for something far beyond this earthly life. Scripture tells us that through Christ, we become heirs to the Kingdom of Heaven (Romans 8:17). This means that as followers of Jesus, we inherit the promises of eternal life, peace, and joy that are found in God's presence.

Though our physical bodies will one day die, that isn't the end of our story. Jesus Himself promised that those who believe in Him will experience resurrection, just as He was raised from the dead (John 11:25–26). Death no longer has the final say. Because of Christ's victory over death, we can be confident that we, too, will be raised to new life, to live forever alongside Him in His Kingdom.

This truth gives us hope and purpose in the present. Even though we live in a world filled with suffering, pain, and death, we know that our time here is temporary. Our true home is in Heaven, and our relationship with Christ guarantees that we will one day live in perfect harmony with Him for eternity. This changes how we view life. Knowing our ultimate destination is eternal life with Christ should give us peace and motivate us to live for His Kingdom now. Our faith in Christ not only secures our future but also shapes our lives today.

There is power in declaring things out loud. Speak life over your fears. Proclaim death to anxiety, fear, and doubt, and pray fervently for the Holy Spirit to speak through you. When we surrender and allow Him to take over, we'll find that we are not bound by our own limitations, but we're empowered by God's strength.

One of the biggest issues with Christians today is that people may confess faith, but they aren't willing to die to themselves. They hold onto their old identities instead of surrendering them and following the Holy Spirit. Jesus said in Matthew 6:24, *"No one can serve two masters."* You can't serve both yourself and Christ. As John 3:3 says, *"Very truly I tell you, no one can see the kingdom of God unless they are born again."* That was the burden on my heart when I wrote this song.

Here are some other Scriptural references within the lyrics:

- "I died that day on the cross with Him, it's He who pays my wage of sin"
    - Concept: Refers to the idea that believers share in the death of Christ which is related to the belief in Jesus's atonement for sin
    - Scripture References:
        - Romans 6:6, "We know that our old self was crucified with him in order that the body of sin might be brought to nothing, so that we would no longer be enslaved to sin" (ESV).
        - Romans 6:23 "For the wages of sin is death, but the free gift of God is eternal life in Christ Jesus our Lord" (ESV).

- "This world hurts, but Jesus saves"
  - Concept: The idea of salvation through Jesus is a central theme in Christianity
  - Scripture Reference:
    - John 3:17, "For God did not send his Son into the world to condemn the world, but in order that the world might be saved through him" (ESV).

- "If you're saved by His grace, you'll never see the grave"
  - Concept: The promise of eternal life for believers
  - Scripture Reference:
    - John 11:25–26, "Jesus said to her, 'I am the resurrection and the life. Whoever believes in me, though he die, yet shall he live, and everyone who lives and believes in me shall never die'" (ESV).

- "I was living in death, but He gave me life"
  - Concept: Spiritual rebirth and the gift of eternal life through Christ
  - Scripture Reference:
    - John 10:10, "The thief comes only to steal and kill and destroy. I came that they may have life and have it abundantly" (ESV).

- "His return will be like a thief in the night"
  - Scripture Reference:
    - 1 Thessalonians 5:2, "For you yourselves are fully aware that the day of the Lord will come like a thief in the night" (ESV).

- "Jesus said, follow Me and I'll lead you to rest"
  - Scripture Reference:
    - Matthew 11:28, "Come to me, all who labor and are heavy laden, and I will give you rest" (ESV).

- "Amazing grace, trumps selfish pride"
  - Concept: The transformative power of grace over pride
  - Scripture Reference:
    - Ephesians 2:8–9, "For by grace you have been saved through faith. And this is not your own doing; it is the gift of God, not a result of works, so that no one may boast" (ESV).

- "I was a thief on the cross, dying by His side"
  - Scripture Reference:
    - Luke 23:39–43, "One of the criminals who were hanged railed at him, saying, 'Are you not the Christ? Save yourself and us!' But the other rebuked him, saying, 'Do you not fear God, since you are under the same sentence of condemnation? And we indeed justly; for we are receiving the due reward of our deeds; but this man has done nothing wrong.' And he said, 'Jesus, remember me when you come into your kingdom.' And he said to him, 'Truly, I say to you, today you will be with me in paradise'" (ESV).

Forever Changed

*"For God so loved the world, that he gave his only begotten Son,
that whosoever believeth in him should not perish,
but have everlasting life.
For God sent not his Son into the world to condemn the world;
but that the world through him might be saved.
He that believeth on him is not condemned"* (John 3:16–18, KJV).

Faith, hope, and His love, all the gifts from God above
Every sin is washed in blood, saved like Noah from the flood.
He's all God all Man, this has always been the plan,

Ever since time began, I know it's hard to understand,
He's crucified on the cross, saved everyone who's lost
Take a moment, let that pause, place it heavy in your thoughts,
I owe it all, all to Christ, He blessed me with a godly wife,
I was dead, brought to life, I was blind, He gave me sight
He blessed me with two sons, looked at death and said, I won.
Gave me breath inside my lungs, understand when I speak in tongues
Christ is knocking at the door, promising not to hurt anymore
Bow your head to the floor and say with me, thank you, Lord

[Chorus]
Lead me to the cross, Lord, take away my pain
I know I've been so lost, Lord, cleanse me in Your name
You have paid the cost, Lord, break away these chains
You're always in my thoughts, Lord, I'm forever changed

Sit and listen, let me tell you about the God I love
The One who came down from the heavens above
He gave His life, He sacrificed, in the darkness, He's a light
He paid the price for all the evil things that we've done
It's beyond easy to become Christ's disciple,
When all you gotta do is pick up the Holy Bible
Give up your false idols that make you feel entitled
You're going through denial, but His love is never rivaled
Meditate, pray, and try to open your mind
Then you'll be surprised at the peace that you find
Christ is coming in time, but tell me what will He find
Depressed and broken flesh or a soul that shines

[Chorus]

The older I get, the sweeter He gets, wrapped in His silhouette
Understand why Jesus wept, the price He paid for our debt
He knows how much we suffer, like a child without a mother
His mercy's bread and butter, like our love of Christian brothers
I'm lost, sometimes I fall, like runnin' into a brick wall
Till I hear my Father call, Jesus said, I'll take it all
Let His Spirit save your soul, learn to give up your control
Grab His hand and take a hold, see how fast He makes you whole

Never doubt that He will win, wash away every sin
All you need is to repent, 'cause of Him your soul is cleansed
Raise your hands, give Him praise,
Glory to the One who's raised from the dead in three days
Thank you, Jesus, now I'm saved
(Now I'm saved)
(Now I'm saved)
(Thank You, Jesus, now I'm saved)

Behind the Song

"FOREVER CHANGED" WAS THE second song I wrote and recorded. My thought process during this one was a bit scattered—I knew I was following a calling, but I was still trying to figure out my direction. During the writing process, I blended personal testimony, Scripture, and the wisdom I wanted to share with the listener. Despite the nervousness I felt throughout the process, I think the song turned out great.

The song opens with the powerful message of John 3:16, a verse that has resonated with countless believers and is often regarded as the cornerstone of the Christian faith: *"For God so loved the world, that he gave his only begotten Son, that whosoever believeth in him should not perish, but have everlasting life."* This verse is more than familiar Scripture—it encapsulates the heart of the Gospel, the very essence of God's love and His desire to save humanity.

John 3:16 is well-known because it speaks about the depth of God's love in a way that is both simple and profound. It tells us that God's love isn't just a distant, abstract concept—it's personal, active, and sacrificial. By sending His only Son—Jesus Christ—to die for our sins, God demonstrated the greatest act of love imaginable, bridging the gap between sinful humanity and Himself. This act was motivated by God's deep desire to save us, to rescue us from eternal separation from Him, and to invite us into a personal, intimate relationship with Him.

The beauty of John 3:16 lies in its invitation to everyone—regardless of who they are or what they've done, God's love is available to all who believe in Jesus. It's a love that doesn't demand perfection but simple faith, offering eternal life and the promise of a relationship with our Creator. Though often memorized and quoted, this verse is a profound reminder that God's love is not just for the future in eternity, but it is an invitation to experience His love and grace in our daily lives—here and now.

By starting the song with this verse, it creates a clear message: God's love is the foundation—the reason we can find hope, salvation, and the strength to walk in faith. It's an invitation to reflect on the overwhelming, sacrificial love of God and the depth of His desire to have a relationship with each of us.

The fact that Christ came to save and teach us—and then willingly went to the cross—should never be something we simply acknowledge and move on from—it deserves a permanent place in our hearts, minds, and daily thoughts. His sacrifice is the very foundation of our faith—the reason we have hope, forgiveness, and eternal life. This wasn't just a historical event; it's a life-changing truth that shapes how we live each and every day.

When we remember that Christ came to earth with a purpose—to rescue us from sin, death, and eternal separation from Him—it reminds us of how precious we are to God. Jesus didn't just offer teachings to help us live better lives; He provided a way for us to be reconciled to God through His death and resurrection. His teachings guide us toward living in alignment with God's will, but it is His sacrifice on the cross that secures our redemption. Without His willingness to lay down His life, we would still be lost in sin.

Keeping this truth at the forefront of our minds helps us remain grounded in our faith. It's easy to become distracted by the demands of daily life or to be consumed by temporary struggles, but reflecting on Christ's sacrifice reminds us of the bigger picture. He endured the cross for us out of His immense love and desire to offer us eternal life. This awareness should shape our responses to difficulties and temptations, as well as how we treat others, knowing the lengths Jesus went to show us grace.

In the chorus of the song, when I ask God to lead me to the cross and break away my chains, it's a prayer of surrender and freedom. The cross represents the ultimate place of sacrifice and redemption where Jesus laid down His life to break the power of sin and death over us. Asking to be led to the cross is a call to be drawn closer to that redemptive moment, to be reminded of the incredible love and grace that was poured out for us.

The chains I speak of represent the burdens, sins, and struggles that have held me back—whether it's fear, doubt, guilt, or any form of bondage that keeps me from living in the fullness of Christ's freedom. By calling on God to break these chains, I'm acknowledging that only He has the power to release me from what has held me captive. It's not something I can do on my own; I need His intervention.

God has carried me through so much in life, through trials and storms, even when I couldn't see His hand at work. He has always been there to lead me, even during the times when I wasn't following Him as closely as I should have. Despite my own shortcomings or missteps, His faithfulness has never wavered. He has always been present, patiently guiding me, waiting for the moment I would fully turn to Him.

Once I finally surrendered and found my way to Him, my life was forever changed. It wasn't just a temporary shift, but it was a complete transformation. Encountering God at the cross brought a new perspective, a new heart, and a new purpose. It's like stepping into the light after wandering in the dark—everything looks different, clearer, and more meaningful. The burdens I carried no longer weighed me down the same way because I realized that Christ had already carried them for me. My identity was no longer tied to my past or my mistakes, but to the freedom and new life I found in Him.

Starting the path of discipleship is the easy part—it's the excitement of a new beginning, the eagerness to grow in faith. But the real challenge lies in staying committed, day after day, as the trials and distractions of life try to pull us off course. However, if we truly devote ourselves to spending time in God's Word, making prayer a regular conversation with Him, and reflecting on His teachings, then the journey becomes not only possible but deeply rewarding. It's through these daily disciplines that our faith matures, and we grow stronger in our walk with Christ.

In the song, I share pieces of my personal testimony—how God completely transformed my life, blessing me with a godly wife and two sons who are true gifts from Him. One line that holds a special place in my heart is, "The older I get, the sweeter He gets." This resonates deeply with me because, as the years go by, my relationship with God only grows richer. With age comes not only wisdom but also a deeper faith, and the more I experience His grace and mercy, the more I am in awe of His goodness.

When I'm feeling lost, I can still hear my Father's voice calling me. In John 10:27, Jesus says, *"My sheep listen to my voice; I know them, and they follow me."* This verse reminds us that no matter what we face in life, His voice is always there, guiding us back to Him. Even in the darkest or most confusing moments, if we pause and listen, we will hear His call and find our way. He knows us intimately and is always ready to lead us if we just follow Him.

When I wrote the song, I was still learning how to blend lyrics with personal testimony and the Scriptures that mean the most to me. It wasn't a polished process—my thoughts were a bit scattered, and there were moments of vulnerability and uncertainty. But in those moments of wrestling with the words, I believe the authenticity of my heart shines through. My prayer is that, despite any imperfections, the song reflects my genuine desire for people to be open to the love and saving grace of Jesus Christ.

Through the ups and downs of the writing process, I kept coming back to the goal of helping others see that Christ can make them new, just as He did for me. I didn't want the song to be just about my story, but a tool that could point listeners to the Lord. I want people to feel invited to experience God's transformative power in their own lives and understand that no matter where they are in life, He is waiting for them with open arms.

A neat story that came from this song is how I formed a relationship with a Nigerian artist named Samuna. He reached out to tell me how much he liked "Forever Changed" and asked to do a remix of it in his native language so he could share it with the people in his region of Nigeria. I gave him permission and even funded the project for him. Normally, people would be wary of such requests—especially from Nigeria, given the stigma surrounding scams, but something in my gut told me to trust him.

Several months later, the seed I planted bore fruit—he released a version of "Forever Changed," and it sounds absolutely beautiful. In fact, I think it might even sound better than my original version. This step of faith not only formed a lifelong friendship with another artist who is passionate about his walk with God, but it also spread the message of the song to a new audience in Nigeria and the surrounding areas.

Some of the key lyrics and Scriptures I used in this song include:

- "I was blind, He gave me sight"
  - Scripture Reference:
    - John 9:25, "He replied, 'Whether He is a sinner or not, I don't know. One thing I do know: I was blind but now I see!'"
  - Comment: This verse resonates deeply with me because, for years, I believed in Jesus, but I was still spiritually blind. It wasn't until I sought a personal relationship with Him that I could finally see clearly for the first time.

- "Christ is knocking at the door"
  - Scripture Reference:
    - Revelation 3:20, "Here I am! I stand at the door and knock. If anyone hears my voice and opens the door, I will come in and eat with that person, and they with me."

  Comment: I love this verse because it shows how close Christ is to us. He's right on the other side of the door, waiting for us to simply open it and receive His gift of salvation. We often overcomplicate something that really is so simple.

- "He gave His life, He sacrificed"
  - Scripture Reference:
    - John 3:16, "For God so loved the world that He gave His one and only Son, that whoever believes in Him shall not perish but have eternal life."
  - Comment: This Scripture hits me hard as a father of two sons. I love them dearly, and I can't imagine the pain God the Father felt watching His Son go through so much torment for our sakes. It reveals a depth of love that's beyond our human understanding.

- "Jesus wept"
  - Scripture reference:
    - John 11:35, which simply says, "Jesus wept."
  - Comment: This is the shortest verse in the Bible, but it carries immense power and emotion. It shows the humanity of Jesus—that He felt and experienced the same emotions that we do.

- "Jesus said, 'I'll take it all'"
  - Scripture reference:
    - Matthew 11:28–30, "Come to Me, all you who are weary and burdened, and I will give you rest. Take My yoke upon you and learn from Me, for I am gentle and humble in heart, and you will find rest for your souls. For My yoke is easy and My burden is light."
  - Comment: This verse is profound. We spend so much of our lives weighed down by burdens, yet Jesus offers to take all of that from us. Imagine the freedom of releasing the very things that have been breaking us for so long and allowing Him to carry them instead.

- "Glory to the One who's raised from the dead in three days"
    - Scripture Reference:
        - Luke 24:46, "This is what is written: The Messiah will suffer and rise from the dead on the third day."
    - Comment: I close the song with this powerful affirmation—that Christ fulfilled prophecies written hundreds of years before His coming. As 1 Corinthians 15:14 says, "And if Christ has not been raised, our preaching is useless and so is your faith." The apostles died proclaiming the testimony that Jesus Christ is the Messiah.

Childlike Faith

Jesus loves me, I know, Bible tells me so

[Chorus]
You wanna be Christ-like, gotta have childlike (Faith)
Consider it a trial by faith, living in His grace
Take the Father's hands, welcome His embrace
The world's a better place with childlike (Faith)
 You wanna be Christ-like, gotta have childlike (Faith)
Consider it a trial by faith, living in His grace

Take the Father's hands, welcome His embrace
The world's a better place with childlike (Faith)

Life is so simple through the eyes of a child
A simple smile can let your sense of wonder run wild
Creativity that's never tainted and undefiled
I came with open arms and You looked at me and smiled
My body grows old, but my spirit gets younger
When I slip and fall, You pick me up and I recover
I'm filled with Your spirit so my soul never hungers
You're my Teacher, my Father, my heavenly Instructor
It's common sense, maybe that's why I feel so confident
We know that every action will be followed with a consequence
Wasting our days will only lead to the bottomless
I don't want retirement reflecting on the time we spent
Every breath's reminding me that Your truth won't hide from me
Blessings You supply to me seem to multiply to me
That's why I'm mystified, You see, trust You can rely on me
With child-like faith, heaven has a place set aside for me

[Chorus]

Lord, I'm childlike and You fill me with imagination
Your creations are worthy of our fascination
You gave us 66 love letters through dictation
With a clear message, no matter the interpretation
The remedy is to love your neighbor so it's clear to me
Embracing those that sin while rejecting negativity
Idolatry and bigotry, I don't let those things get to me
On bended knee, I beg the Holy Spirit come and live in me
So, to You I applaud, every breath and every thought
The Gospel is abroad and not a single word is flawed
I can always find protection in Your staff and rod
You cleaned me and saved me from the life of a fraud
Overwhelmed by sin and only speaking in my ignorance
I'd rather worship at Your feet in awe of Your opulence
It helps me to recompense knowing that You're heaven sent
And Father, when I'm lost, You help lead me to deliverance

[Chorus]

Childlike, Lord, I look at You in awe and wonder
Your grace is amazing, Your voice is known to thunder
When I read Your word, I never know what I'll discover
I know that Your love couldn't be replaced with another
So lead me, guide me with anticipation
Open up my eyes, let me see Your revelation
Show this generation Your holy invitation
And make their reservation to heaven's destination
Trust the one that died for me, forgive the ones that lied to me
Open up my eyes and see that Your light's inside of me
Punish those that blinded me, praise to those that guided me
Mercy is applied to me, I know that You'll provide for me
180 in my life made people think of me as odd
I'd rather be judged different than portray a façade
You're all that I got, my ticket to heaven's been bought
With child-like faith, that's why we're called children of God

[Chorus x2]

Behind the Song

"CHILDLIKE FAITH" WAS THE third song I wrote and recorded. It is inspired by Matthew 18:2–5, which says:

> *"He called a little child to Him and placed the child among them. And He said, 'Truly I tell you, unless you change and become like little children, you will never enter the kingdom of heaven. Therefore, whoever takes the lowly position of this child is the greatest in the kingdom of heaven. And whoever welcomes one such child in My name welcomes Me.'"*

I felt a special kind of excitement when this track came together, as it wasn't just any ordinary recording—it became a part of family legacy. At just four years old, my older son sang the introduction and part of the chorus. For me, as a father, it was an incredibly proud moment. Featuring his voice on the track enabled me to capture a piece of his childhood forever. I can listen to his pure, innocent voice that is full of faith, and hold onto that memory of his youth no matter how old he gets. More than a recording, this song reflects a time when my son's childlike belief in Christ was so fresh and simple. Knowing that this moment is sealed in the song forever fills my heart with a joy that words can hardly express. Having created this connection between the music, our family, and our shared faith is something that I'll always cherish.

The only way to draw closer to God and cultivate a deeper relationship with Him is by approaching Him with a heart of humility, wonder, and innocence—much like a child. Jesus Himself said in Matthew 18:3, "Unless you change and become like little children, you will never enter the kingdom of heaven." A child approaches life with awe, trust, and dependency, unclouded by pride or doubt. In the same way, we are called to approach God with a sense of openness, free of preconceived notions or the burdens of self-reliance. When we come before Him with childlike faith, we leave room for His guidance, comfort, and wisdom to flow into our lives.

This posture of childlike wonder allows us to see God's work with fresh eyes and marvel at His goodness, power, and grace. It strips away the cynicism and jadedness that often cloud our spiritual journey. Just as a child seeks comfort in the presence of a loving parent, we are invited to lean fully into God's love, trusting that He cares for us deeply and knows what is best. Only through this surrendered trust can we experience the fullness of His presence and grow in intimacy with Him.

Though my body grows older and weaker with time, my spirit becomes younger and more vibrant as I draw closer to Christ. The aches and pains in my body—whether it's my back or my knees—remind me of my physical limitations, but my spirit is being renewed daily. As I gain a deeper revelation of how to walk with Christ, life becomes simpler—filled with peace and joy that transcend the trials of life. This spiritual renewal gives me a childlike heart, eager to learn, grow closer to God, and marvel at His goodness.

Jesus said in Matthew 11:30 that His yoke is easy and His burden is light. As I grow in my walk with Him, I realize the truth in this promise. The complexities of life that once weighed me down no longer have the same power over me, because my focus has shifted to what truly matters—my relationship with God. My spirit is young, filled with wonder and anticipation for the things He has yet to reveal. Though my body ages, my heart is light, unburdened, and filled with the joy of a child who delights in the presence of his Heavenly Father. The closer I get to Christ, the more I am reminded that this life is just the beginning of an eternal journey—one where the spirit never ages and the joy never fades.

Jesus serves multiple roles in my life—Teacher, Father, and heavenly Instructor. As my Teacher, He imparts wisdom and guidance through His Word, offering profound lessons that challenge me to grow in faith and understanding. His parables and sermons serve as a roadmap for navigating life's complexities, illuminating the path to righteousness and encouraging me to live according to God's will.

As my Father, Jesus shows me unconditional love, support, and care. He is my comfort in times of distress and my protector in life's storms. Just as an earthly father desires the best for his children, Jesus longs for me to experience a life with purpose and fulfillment. His embrace is a reminder that I am never alone; He walks alongside me, encouraging me to lean on Him in my struggles, while rejoicing with Him in my victories.

As my heavenly Instructor, Jesus leads me toward spiritual maturity. He challenges me to reflect on my beliefs and actions, urging me to seek a deeper relationship with God. His teachings are not merely historical accounts; they are living principles that resonate with my everyday experiences. Through prayer and Scripture, I am continually reminded of His desire to instruct me, helping me to discern right from wrong and guiding me in the decisions I face.

God has gifted us with sixty-six love letters, each filled with His wisdom, guidance, and deep affection for us. Unfortunately, many overlook the beauty of the Bible, and consider reading it a chore rather than a treasure. But when we approach Scripture with a mindset of gratitude and curiosity, it transforms our experience. Instead of viewing it as an obligation, we can embrace it as a wonderful opportunity to connect with God.

When we take the time to read and reflect on its pages, the Bible comes alive in our hearts and minds. Stories of faith, perseverance, and divine love unfold before us, revealing insights that can profoundly impact our lives. Each verse is a testament to God's unwavering love and teaches us about His character and His desires for us.

When we shift our perspective, we can discover that the Bible is not just a book but a source of encouragement, comfort, and inspiration. It invites us into a deeper relationship with God and helps us discover His purpose for our lives. When we view the Bible as a blessing, we open ourselves up to a deeper appreciation for its messages, allowing them to resonate within us and shape our journey of faith. Let's cherish these love letters and allow their wisdom to enrich our lives.

Have you ever witnessed a child who is bold and fearless? Their confidence stems from knowing they are safe and protected in their environment. In the same way, as children of God, we can approach life without fear. Jesus is our Shepherd, and we are His flock. Just as a shepherd provides shelter, food, and safety for his sheep, Jesus watches over us, guiding and protecting us through life's challenges. When we trust in His care, we can face each day with courage, confident that He is always present to lead and watch over us. This assurance allows us to navigate the uncertainties of life with faith rather than fear. By fully embracing our relationship with Jesus, we can face obstacles head-on, reflecting the boldness of a child who knows he is safe and loved.

This transformation in my life has caused those around me who were accustomed to the person I used to be to see me as odd or strange. And do you know what? That's perfectly okay with me. I would much rather be perceived this way than return to my old ways. Embracing this new lifestyle rooted in faith has revealed which relationships truly matter—the ones grounded in genuine love and support. As I have drawn closer to the Lord with childlike faith, I have come to realize that we are not all children of God. This journey has not only changed me but also deepened my understanding of love and connection. The people who remain by my side—those who encourage me in my faith and celebrate my transformation—are the ones who truly love me for who I am now, not for who I once was.

This shift in perspective allows me to cherish the beauty of my faith-filled life, knowing that I am part of a loving family that transcends earthly ties. Each day, I embrace my identity as a child of God, finding joy in this new path and in the relationships that flourish because of it.

Several Scriptures inspired the lyrics and message of "Childlike Faith," such as:

- "Jesus loves me, I know the Bible tells me so"
    - Concept: this reflects the essence of childlike faith that Jesus taught.
    - Scripture Reference:
        - 1 John 4:19, "We love because He first loved us."

- "Take the Father's hands, welcome His embrace"
  - Scripture Reference:
    - Isaiah 41:13, "For I am the Lord your God who takes hold of your right hand and says to you, 'Do not fear; I will help you.'"

- "You cleanse me and save me from the life of a fraud"
  - Scripture Reference:
    - 1 John 1:9, "If we confess our sins, He is faithful and just and will forgive us our sins and purify us from all unrighteousness."

- "With childlike faith, that's why we're called children of God"
  - Scripture Reference:
    - John 1:12, "Yet to all who did receive Him, to those who believed in His name, He gave the right to become children of God."

Son of No One

[Chorus]
I was the son of no one, until the day You saved me
I was the son of no one, until the day You saved me
I was lost in this world, alone in this world
It all changed because You claimed me,
Lost in this world, alone in this world
It all changed because You claimed me,
You claimed me, You claimed me
You claimed me, thank God, You claimed me.

My father left when I was only two years old
I'll never understand how a man can be so bold
To leave a child feeling cold, anxious and alone

Without a father in the house, it doesn't feel like a home
I was blinded by my darkness,
Blinded by my hate
I had his last name, but I could never see his face
Through the pain I grew strong,
My direction was all wrong
Wanting a place to belong,
I was closed and withdrawn
I felt so lost, I wasn't wanted as a son
Rejected in life, looking for a father in anyone
One day it all changed, I was finally claimed
When I opened up the Bible, I heard Jesus call my name

[Chorus]

So now let me tell you about the next part of my life
I was completely reborn when I found Jesus Christ
He taught me how to be patient, filled me with His light
Taught me how to love a woman and the ways to treat her right
Now I may have never learned the proper way to fix a car
But You showed me that Your grace can always fix a broken heart
He's the Father of the fatherless,
Savior of the bottomless, leader of the populous,
Keeper of his promises, so now that I'm the father,
I'm gonna do things proper, lead my children to the Altar,
Read Your word like a scholar
I wanna say I love You Lord, I know that You saved me
Jesus, You're my Father and I'm proud that You claimed me

[Chorus]

I was young when you walked away,
It affected me in the worst way
Felt no worth,
Didn't call on my birthdays,
Just the first phase
Now I'm feeling weak,
Everyday blends together like last week
Truth is I'm beat, if you could you would repeat
And leave me alone, chilling in that Datsun 210
We called home,

In the Beginning

I needed a man, I needed my dad
You was absent, I was feeling it bad,
You sealed my path, and I'm really glad,
Got the love of the Father only God had
Reserved for me, like surgery

[Chorus]

Behind the Song

"SON OF NO ONE" WAS MY FOURTH track released, and it's a deeply personal song about my experience of growing up without a father. The song highlights one of the many talents of Piero Digilio. I started by writing the chorus and recorded a rough take to give him an idea of the direction I wanted the song to go. When I say rough, I mean it was hard to listen to—it was purely to communicate the concept. Within just a few days, Piero created the instrumental, and I was blown away by how professional it sounded, especially considering how quickly he had made it. While working on it, he advised me that I needed to start collaborating with other artists. That got me looking through Christian artist Facebook groups, and I connected with an artist named ProphetiQ.

We struck up a friendship as we listened to each other's music and developed a mutual respect for one other's love of serving the Lord. I pitched the idea to him of collaborating on "Son of No One," and he loved it—especially since he had gone through a similar experience. I sent him the beat, and we both went to work on our verses.

When I began writing this song, I knew I didn't want it to be just about the pain of growing up without a father. I wanted it to also offer hope to others since I found healing through embracing Jesus Christ as my Father. The chorus captures this idea: "I was the son of no one, until the day You claimed me. I was lost in this world, alone in this world, but it all changed because You claimed me." That was my personal declaration. I had always believed in Jesus, but I didn't know how to have a personal relationship with Him as a child. Even still, His teachings and Scriptures laid the foundation for my morality—something most children learn from their father.

The first verse delves into the impact of growing up without a father—a reality that shaped my entire childhood and the way I viewed myself. My biological father left when I was only two, leaving behind not just an empty chair at the table but a profound emptiness in my heart that affected every part of my life. Without his presence, my home felt incomplete, as though a key piece of my identity was missing. I spent years grappling with that void, trying to understand why I wasn't enough to make him want to stay.

As I grew older, I became consumed by feelings of anger and bitterness. Every time I heard other kids talk about their dads—sharing stories of fishing trips, words of wisdom, and those fatherly moments that seemed so essential—it was a harsh reminder of what I never had. When they spoke of their fathers like they were superheroes, the admiration in their voices cut deep. Their joy was my sorrow, a constant, painful reminder of the love I never received.

What made it even worse was when people pointed out how much I looked like him. To them, it was just an innocent observation, but to me, it felt like the ultimate insult. How could I bear any resemblance to the man who had abandoned me? Their words seemed to link me to the very source of my pain. Being compared to the man who had chosen to leave became a wound I carried for years, a constant struggle to separate who I was from the father who wasn't there.

Bearing the last name that belonged to a man who had chosen to walk away from my life weighed on me like a heavy burden—an invisible but ever-present reminder of rejection. Every time I heard my own name, I couldn't shake the feeling that it was a label tied to someone who wanted nothing to do with me. That hurt seeped into my spirit, fueling my anger.

I found myself gravitating toward older men in my life, hoping to find in them the guidance, wisdom, and love that I had missed out on. I reached out in silent desperation, searching for someone to show me how to navigate life as a man. This quest became both a blessing and a curse. It was a curse because it often ended in disappointment. Those I reached out to couldn't fill the role I longed for, leaving me feeling even more hopeless and lost than before. That constant sense of rejection deepened my wounds and made it hard for me to trust anyone.

This unresolved hurt shaped my view of myself and others. I didn't just feel abandoned by my father; I felt rejected as a person, and I carried that weight into every relationship and decision I made. The bitterness grew like a poison, making it hard for me to trust, love, or even believe that I was worthy of being loved. Yet amidst that struggle, there were moments of blessing. One of the greatest came from my grandfather. He didn't just offer me advice or comfort—he handed me something that would change the course of my life forever: my first Bible. That moment was pivotal, though I didn't realize its full significance right away. The Bible wasn't just a book; it was a doorway to something far greater than any earthly father figure could offer.

For the first time, I felt like I had been given a map to navigate the confusion and pain that had long plagued my heart. This wasn't guidance from just a man; it was the eternal wisdom of my Heavenly Father. The anger that used as fuel my bitterness began to transform as I entered into a deep search for peace, healing, and understanding. I realized that my earthly father's absence didn't have to define my identity or my future. Within the pages of that Bible, I found the reassurance that I wasn't alone—that I was seen, known, and loved by a Father who would never abandon me. That moment marked the beginning of my journey from hurt and anger to healing and redemption.

The Bible became more than just a gift—it became the foundation of my transformation. Through it, I learned that no matter how broken my earthly relationships were, I had a Father in Heaven who called me His own. This realization filled the void left by my biological father and gave me a new sense of purpose. What had once been a source of pain—the last name I carried—now served as a testament to how far God had brought me, leading me from despair to hope, from abandonment to being fully embraced by His love.

While I had heard stories of Jesus and attended church, this moment was different. Holding that Bible in my hands for the first time, I felt something shift within me. Now, I could dive into His words and absorb their meaning for myself, not just through someone else's interpretation or in the confines of a Sunday service. I could explore His teachings, reflect on His parables, and begin to understand the life He lived and the love He showed. As I read through the pages of the Bible, Jesus became more than just a distant figure from history; He became my role model, someone I could look up to. Even though I didn't fully grasp His divinity at such a young age, I was drawn to His example of compassion, humility, and service—caring for the poor, the sick, and the downtrodden. His life was marked by a kindness and strength that resonated deep within me.

Growing up in a rough neighborhood, I frequently found myself doing things just to fit in with the crowd. I became entangled in behaviors and choices that, deep down, I knew weren't right. The pressure to conform was real, and I didn't want to stand out or be seen as weak. But despite the choices I made, there was always this guiding light, a persistent whisper in the back of my mind reminding me of Jesus and His teachings. It was as if no matter how far I strayed, His example lingered, encouraging me that there was another way to live—one grounded in love, not fear.

Looking back, I can genuinely say I don't know who I'd be today if my grandfather hadn't gifted me that Bible. That small but significant gesture was the catalyst that set me on a path toward healing and self-discovery. It was as if God had handed me a lifeline in the form of His Word, guiding me away from destructive paths and toward the life He had intended for me all along.

The second verse of the song shifts to my life today, reflecting on how I found a real relationship with Jesus when my oldest son was born. At that time, I was in a dark place—having just lost my home to foreclosure and battling multiple health issues that left me reliant on a cane. I knew I didn't want to continue living that way, especially not in front of my son. That realization brought me to my knees. I broke down and surrendered everything to God, laying my burdens, stress, and anxiety at His feet. In that moment, I felt the old, sick me died and I was reborn in Christ.

Once I made that decision, everything changed. I became active again and for the first time in a long time, I could walk and run without a cane. I felt like a new man—someone my son could look up to with pride. My newfound faith lit a path before me and began teaching me invaluable lessons: how to love my wife deeply and how to lead my family with both intention and grace.

One of my favorite lines from the song encapsulates this journey: "Now I may have never learned the proper way to fix a car, but You showed me that Your grace can always fix a broken heart." This line speaks volumes about the lessons the Lord has taught me, especially in the areas that truly matter. While I may not have mastered tasks traditionally associated with manhood—like fixing cars or handling tools—God has shown me something far more profound. His grace has taught me how to fix what is broken within the human heart, starting with my own.

Many men pride themselves on excelling in those "manly" tasks, and there's nothing wrong with that. Being capable of practical, hands-on skills is valuable, and I admire those who can build things or repair what is physically broken. But I've come to realize that there's an even greater kind of strength needed—one that doesn't rely on physical tools, but on spiritual ones. I've met men who are skilled with their hands but struggle deeply in areas that require emotional depth, compassion, and love—areas that are essential to nurturing a family, a marriage, or even a relationship with their children.

The truth is, fixing a broken car can't compare to the task of fixing a broken heart. And it's in these places of the heart—where anger, bitterness, and fear reside—that Christ's grace does its most powerful work. When I reflect on my own journey with God, I see how His grace has not only healed my heart but also equipped me to be a better husband and father. Christ has taught me values that far exceed the practical skills many men chase after. Through Him, I've learned the importance of patience, humility, forgiveness, and unconditional love.

The morals and values I've learned from Christ have become the foundation of my life, and I wouldn't trade them for anything this world could offer. His teachings on how to love, forgive, and lead my family in faith have given me a strength that no set of tools could ever provide. It's easy to admire those who are self-reliant in the practical sense, but Christ has shown me that true strength is found in extending grace, loving deeply, and nurturing spiritual growth in the lives of those around me.

Now, as a father of two boys, I can't fathom the thought of abandoning them. The love I feel for my sons transcends anything I ever imagined possible. It's a love that's deeper than I ever expected—unconditional, unwavering, and pure. There's a profound sense of responsibility and connection that anchors me; nothing in this world could keep me from being there for them. As I look into their eyes, I see their innocence, trust, and expectation of a father's love, and that is a bond I will never break. Each day, I strive to be the kind of father who fulfills the role my own dad chose to forgo as I commit to providing the love and guidance that I longed for as a child.

I'm determined to do things right. I want my children to never feel a lack of love or support and to know that I am always there for them—no matter what. I endeavor to create an environment where my children feel secure, valued, and cherished, because I believe a father's love is one of the first reflections of God's love a child can experience. In my heart, I want to be that reflection, to show them what it means to be cared for and protected, just as Christ loves and protects us.

I strive to demonstrate the love of Jesus in every action. From the way I discipline with patience to the way I show affection, my goal is to mirror the compassion and understanding that Christ has shown me. My children see me pray every night, and now, my oldest son joins me in those prayers. It's one of the most humbling and beautiful experiences as a father—hearing your own child lift his voice in prayer in his own simple, innocent way. He's learning that prayer is our direct connection to God, a practice that grounds us in faith, and I pray it becomes a foundation in his life too.

They watch as I read the Bible daily, and my older son sits beside me, soaking in the lessons and stories of faith. His curiosity leads him to ask questions about the characters and their choices, and I can already see the seeds of spiritual growth taking root in his young heart. Although my younger son is only eighteen months old, I hope to instill the same values in him as well. Right now, he's observing and learning through our daily routines, but I trust that these early experiences are shaping his understanding of what it means to live a life centered on Christ.

We attend church as a family, and my children witness my excitement during worship and fellowship. It's important to me that they not only hear about faith but see it lived out. When we sing praises together and gather with others in the body of Christ, their joy mirrors my own, and together we experience the beauty of community and faith. They see the way worship brings me peace and fulfillment, and I pray that as they grow, they too will feel the same connection to God through these moments.

I conclude the second verse with a heartfelt expression of gratitude for Christ and everything He has done for me. His love has transformed my life in ways I could never fully describe. He took my brokenness and made me whole, filling the gaps left by my earthly father with His unconditional, divine love. I am forever thankful that I am now a part of His family and that He calls me His own. This reality shapes everything I do as a father, a husband, and a follower of Christ. Knowing that I belong to Him gives me the strength to be the father my sons need, and I pray that through my example, they too will one day experience the life-changing love of Christ.

The third verse, by ProphetiQ, tells his personal testimony. I won't dive too deep into his story because it's not mine to tell, but I can say his verse is emotional and raw. It hits hard. If you haven't heard it, I highly recommend checking it out, as well as some of his other songs.

Overall, this song was a passion project meant to offer hope to those going through similar situations. I wanted to create something that not only reflected my journey but also demonstrated the transformation that can happen when we embrace Christ as our Father. I'm blessed beyond measure. Even though I may be financially poor, I'm spiritually rich, and my family is overflowing with love.

Here are some Scriptures to reflect on while listening to the song.

- "He's the Father of the fatherless"
    - Scripture Reference:
        - Psalm 68:5, "A father to the fatherless, a defender of widows, is God in his holy dwelling."

- "Jesus you're my Father and I'm proud that You claimed me"
  - Implied Scripture Reference:
    - John 1:12, "Yet to all who did receive him, to those who believed in his name, he gave the right to become children of God."

- "Taught me how to love a woman and the ways to treat her right"
  - Implied Scripture Reference:
    - Ephesians 5:25, "Husbands, love your wives, just as Christ loved the church and gave himself up for her."

- "Lead my children to the Altar"
  - Concept: this reflects the call to raise children in the faith
  - Implied Scripture Reference:
    - Proverbs 22:6, "Start children off on the way they should go, and even when they are old they will not turn from it."

- "Keeper of His promises"
  - Concept: this speaks of God's faithfulness
  - Implied Scripture Reference:
    - 2 Peter 3:9, "The Lord is not slow in keeping his promise, as some understand slowness. Instead, he is patient with you, not wanting anyone to perish, but everyone to come to repentance."

Church Hurt

[Chorus]
We've all been broken, some have been by the church
You are His chosen, He'll take away that hurt
Keep your eyes on Him, mind on Him, become immersed
We've all been broken, we are the living Church

Sorry to the church hurt, sorry to the converts
Don't become an introvert, focus on God's work
Fake Christians judge, fake Christians scare
Real Christians love, real Christians care
God's church is greater than a building
'Cause God's love, it can never have a ceiling
I know what you're feeling, I know it's unappealing
Today let's start to healing, see what Christ's revealing

Let your light shine, let it never be undone
Follow the divine, you'll be blinded by no one
Put it all on the line, focus on the Son
'Cause He'll leave the 99, so He can save the one

[Chorus]

His will is sovereign, don't follow doctrines
It's all man-made, those things will fade
Christ will never be forgotten
His arms are open (open)
You may be broken (broken)
Don't be afraid, your soul is saved
Holy Spirit is awoken

My Lord, my God, I need You
My soul's prepared to receive You
I won't grieve, I'm relieved
I can see, what You've achieved
You say You died for me, I believe You

[Chorus]

You're the body of Christ, maintaining spiritual growth
Guard your soul and your mind, let the Holy Spirit invoke
So, prepare for the fight, fill the others with hope
Learn to teach His message right, you're the one that He chose
Your pain is emotional, but hear this devotional
He's broken and crucified, those facts are non-negotiable
He's always approachable, love is unconditional
Humanity is flawed, but Jesus will never be disposable
NOPE

Forgive the ones that hurt
Let Jesus show your worth

[Chorus]

Behind the Song

I FELT COMPELLED TO WRITE "Church Hurt" because it is something I believe nearly everyone experiences at some point in life. When I wrote this, I was in the process of recovering from my own church hurt and was searching for a church home.

The story behind its creation is kind of crazy. After writing the lyrics, I went ahead and booked studio time to record it—only to remember at the last second, that I can't sing! That's when I turned to some Christian artist Facebook groups, looking for a female vocalist willing to record the chorus. At the last minute, the incredible artist, Flawssom, reached out, expressing interest in the song. I sent her the chorus lyrics, and she quickly responded with her vocals. I was blown away—not only by the beauty of her voice but also by her professionalism and willingness to collaborate with a complete stranger. She truly brought the song to life.

As I began writing this song, I was constantly reminded of a familiar quote I've heard among Christians: *"You don't have to go to church to be saved."* While there is undeniable truth in that statement, I've also observed a troubling trend. Many who hold to this belief seem content with merely carrying the title of *"Christian"* without actively pursuing a relationship with God. They neglect reading Scripture or dedicating time for daily prayer. Sadly, this was the mindset I unfortunately adopted throughout my teens and twenties.

A particularly painful church experience led me to develop what I now call a "God wound." I found myself grappling with thoughts like, *"These people who judge me are no better than I am. Who are they to lead a church? I can do this on my own!"* While that mindset felt empowering at the time, it is ultimately dangerous. It fosters isolation and breeds a distorted view of faith. Without the support and fellowship that the church provides, we risk becoming complacent in our spiritual lives. We can easily create a version of Jesus that fits our own beliefs, causing stagnation instead of growth.

In writing this song, my goal was to convey a sense of shared experience with my listeners—to acknowledge the struggles we all face in our spiritual journeys. I've walked through disillusionment and hurt, navigating the rocky terrain of doubts and fears that can lead to feelings of isolation and despair. It's a journey that many can relate to, and by sharing my own experiences, I hope to create a sense of solidarity.

I understand that a single song may not be the catalyst to draw someone back to church or restore their faith, but I wanted to express my empathy for those who have felt lost or abandoned. My intention was to provide a voice for the unspoken struggles that linger beneath the surface and to offer comfort to those who feel alone in their pain. The message of the song is a gentle reminder that it's okay to acknowledge these feelings—many of us have been there, and we're not defined by our struggles.

In my own journey, I encountered various pitfalls that can often ensnare us: cynicism, bitterness, and a disconnection from the very community meant to offer support and healing. Through this song, I aim to help listeners avoid those traps by pointing them toward a deeper connection with God. Faith is more than a set of beliefs or rituals; it's a living, breathing relationship that requires constant nurture and care.

Moreover, I emphasize the significance of a supportive community. It's essential to surround ourselves with those who uplift and encourage us, especially when we feel vulnerable or weary. This song isn't just a reflection of my personal experience, it's also an invitation for others to seek fellowship, engage in honest conversations about faith, and find strength in community. We're meant to walk this journey together, lifting each other up in times of need.

If you find yourself in a similar situation, I encourage you to explore various churches until you discover a good fit. Each congregation has its own unique atmosphere and approach to worship, and you might be surprised by where you feel most at home. If that's not possible, consider starting your own fellowship group. Gather with like-minded individuals who are eager to grow in faith together. And even if neither option is available, remember this profound truth: *you are the Church*. The Holy

Spirit dwells within you, making your heart His temple. When Jesus died, the temple curtain was torn, symbolizing our direct access to God. Now, every believer carries that sacred presence within them.

However, it's crucial to actively live out your faith. If you're not currently attending a church, remember to embody what it means to be the Church. Seek out fellowship with others, share the Gospel, and extend charity and mercy in your daily life. Keep the lines of communication with God open—prayer is how we speak to Him, and Scripture is how He speaks back to us.

I understand that searching for a church home can feel overwhelming, especially when doing it on your own. That's why I encourage you to persist in your search. There's something uniquely special about worshiping and fellowshipping with fellow believers. When you find the right church, the experience can be transformative—it's in those moments that you realize how much you truly needed that community.

Hearing different perspectives and insights from Scripture can open your eyes to truths you may not have recognized before. It enriches your faith journey and deepens your understanding of God's Word.

Don't let a past negative experience keep you from the blessings God has in store for you within a faith community. While I'm not dismissing the real wrongdoings of some churches, my own experiences have taught me that finding the right church can make all the difference. A supportive community can uplift, challenge, and walk alongside you as you navigate your faith. Remember, we are not meant to walk this journey alone; we are called to share it with others.

While writing this song, I had a number of Scriptures in mind:

- "You are His chosen"
    - Concept: a reminder that we are chosen by God
    - Scripture Reference:
        - 1 Peter 2:9, "But you are a chosen people, a royal priesthood, a holy nation, God's special possession."

Modern Psalms, Volume 1

- "He'll take away that hurt"
  - Concept: God's ability to heal and comfort us in times of pain
  - Scripture Reference:
    - Psalm 147:3, "He heals the brokenhearted and binds up their wounds."

- "Keep your eyes on Him"
  - Concept: the importance of focusing on Jesus
  - Scripture Reference:
    - Hebrews 12:2, "Fixing our eyes on Jesus, the pioneer and perfecter of faith."

- "We are the living Church"
  - Concept: believers are the body of Christ.
  - Scripture Reference:
    - 1 Corinthians 12:27, "Now you are the body of Christ, and each one of you is a part of it."

- "Let your light shine"
  - Concept: the call for believers to shine their light before others
  - Scripture Reference:
    - Matthew 5:16, "Let your light shine before others, that they may see your good deeds and glorify your Father in heaven."

- "He'll lead the 99, so He can save the one"
  - Concept: the parable of the lost sheep
  - Scripture Reference:
    - Luke 15:4, "Suppose one of you has a hundred sheep and loses one of them. Doesn't he leave the ninety-nine in the open country and go after the lost sheep until he finds it?"

In the Beginning

- "His will is sovereign"
  - Concept: God's sovereign will over all things
  - Scripture Reference:
    - Romans 9:18, "Therefore God has mercy on whom he wants to have mercy, and he hardens whom he wants to harden."

- "Christ will never be forgotten"
  - Concept: the eternal nature of Christ's reign
  - Scripture Reference:
    - Hebrews 13:8, "Jesus Christ is the same yesterday and today and forever."

- "You say you died for me, I believe you"
  - Concept: the belief in Christ's sacrificial death
  - Scripture Reference:
    - Romans 5:8, "But God demonstrates his own love for us in this: While we were still sinners, Christ died for us."

- "You're the body of Christ"
  - Concept: the Church is the body of Christ
  - Scripture Reference:
    - 1 Corinthians 12:27, "Now you are the body of Christ, and each one of you is a part of it."

- "He's broken and crucified"
  - Concept: Jesus's crucifixion and suffering for our sins
  - Scripture Reference:
    - Isaiah 53:5, "But he was pierced for our transgressions, he was crushed for our iniquities."

- "Forgive the ones that hurt"
  - Concept: the call to forgive others, just as Christ forgave us
  - Scripture Reference:
    - Ephesians 4:32, "Be kind and compassionate to one another, forgiving each other, just as in Christ God forgave you."

Unbreakable Love

[Chorus]
You have found a way to love me, clearly now I see!
(Your love is unbreakable)
Though I walk this road so lonely, truly I am free!
(Your love is unbreakable)
Truly now I'm free!

Fisher of men, living in sin
Learn to repent.
Then born again
I'm so amazed
Life from the grave, sins You forgave
Made me saved

Modern Psalms, Volume 1

Breaker of death, giver of breath
Life is stressed
But You are blessed
(Your love is unbreakable)

Neither death nor life can break me
No angels no demons can shake me
The present and future keep waiting
No high or low can take me
Lead me to be a leader
Teach me to be a teacher
You've turned me into a believer
(Your love is unbreakable)

[Chorus]

God is good all the time
All the time God is good
Bringer of light
Shine so bright
Did what was right
Misunderstood
Walk by faith
To the gates
I await
My brotherhood
(Your love is unbreakable)

No one in this world is more holy
Embrace me in all of Your glory
Every gospel shares Your story
I know You died for me
Lead me forward, You're my shepherd
Free me from worldly tethers
Forever written in record
(Your love is unbreakable)

[Chorus]

In the Beginning

Fill with desire
Spirit's on fire
I'm inspired
Take me higher
I believe
Never deceived
You know my needs
I'll never grieve
Power of prayer
Shows You care
Always aware
Of the cross You bear
(Your love is unbreakable)

It's beyond my understanding
That He is living water
Bless me with Your compassion
Walk with me my Father
King of earth and of heaven
Make me Your disciple
You've heard my confession
(Your love is unbreakable)

[Chorus]

Behind the Song

"UNBREAKABLE LOVE" IS ONE OF my personal favorites. This track also features the incredibly talented Rob Ruff, who has more musical skill in his pinky toe than I could ever hope to have. After finishing my song "Church Hurt," I began searching for fresh inspiration. That's when I thought of asking my wife's grandmother for her favorite Bible verse, intending to use it as the foundation for my next song.

She told me that her favorite verse is Romans 8:38–39, which says:

"For I am convinced that neither death nor life, neither angels nor demons, neither the present nor the future, nor any powers, neither height nor depth, nor anything else in all creation, will be able to separate us from the love of God that is in Christ Jesus our Lord."

I was amazed by her response. Often, when you ask a Christian about their favorite Bible verse, they'll mention a well-known passage like John 3:16. But the verse she mentioned from Romans was so powerful that I knew I had to do it justice.

My wife's grandmother is one of the sweetest women I've ever known, and I wanted to honor her by making this song as beautiful and meaningful as possible. So I reached out to Rob Ruff again, and to my excitement, he agreed to collaborate. I explained the significance of the song with him, Rob wrote and sang the chorus—beautifully, I might add. From there the process was effortless. Rob's work on the chorus set the tone, and I wrote the verses and the bridge.

While creating this song, I drew inspiration from several Scriptures, all of which emphasize the greatness of God's love and how nothing can separate us from it.

I wanted this song to center on the core message of Romans 8:38–39, which reassures us that nothing can separate us from the love of Christ.

However, it was equally important to illustrate *why* this message is true. We must remember that Christ is not just a distant figure; He is the King of kings, the Lord of lords, the Good Shepherd, and the Son of God. His love is so deep, and unconditional that He willingly laid down His life for us. That act of love is the ultimate testament to His character and purpose.

When we reflect on this powerful passage, we must also remember what Christ endured for our sake. His sacrifice was more than the physical act of crucifixion—it was a journey of suffering that included rejection, humiliation, and torture. Jesus was mocked, beaten, and ultimately crucified in one of the most brutal forms of execution known to man. He carried His own cross through the streets, bearing not only the crushing weight of the wood but also the weight of our sins and the anguish of separation from the Father.

Picture it: nails were driven through Jesus's hands and feet, and His body was suspended on the cross—exposed, vulnerable, and enduring the scorn of the very people He came to save. His sacrifice wasn't just for those who followed Him then; but for every single person—past, present, and future. Jesus suffered and died, to remove the barrier of sin that separates us from His love, so that we might be reconciled to God.

Understanding this sacrifice is crucial because it underscores the depth of His commitment to us. Jesus didn't endure such terrible suffering only to abandon us later. His love is eternal, and nothing—no hardship, no sin, no distance—can sever that bond. This is what makes Christianity unique among world religions. In all other belief systems, people strive to earn eternal life through good works or moral living. However, Jesus offered a radically different path: the only way to the Father is through Him—the pure and spotless Lamb of God—who lived a perfect life on our behalf and fulfilled the requirements of the law that we could never accomplish.

The implications of this truth are profound. No matter what challenges we face—whether it's loss, illness, betrayal, or any form of adversity—Christ's love will never fail us. In Him, we are assured that we will never experience abandonment. This promise is the essence of what

I call "Unbreakable Love." It is a love that invites us into a relationship, assuring us that we are cherished and valued just as we are. A love that stands firm through trials, offers solace in sorrow, and invites us to rest in His arms. When the world feels overwhelming, chaotic, or uncertain we can find refuge in the certainty of Christ's love. This message is more than a comforting thought—it is the foundation of our faith, encouraging us to embrace the truth that we are never alone, no matter what we encounter.

Here are some of the key Scriptures that guided me while writing this song:

- "Fisher of men"
  - Concept: Jesus calling His disciples to be "fishers of men"
  - Scripture Reference:
    - Matthew 4:19, "'Come, follow me,' Jesus said, 'and I will send you out to fish for people.'"

- "Learn to repent, then born again"
  - Concept: the importance of repentance and being born again
  - Scripture References:
    - John 3:3, "Jesus replied, '"Very truly I tell you, no one can see the kingdom of God unless they are born again.'"
    - Acts 2:38, "Peter replied, '"Repent and be baptized, every one of you, in the name of Jesus Christ for the forgiveness of your sins.'"

- "Breaker of death, Giver of breath"
  - Concept: Christ's victory over death and God as the giver of life
  - Scripture References:
    - 1 Corinthians 15:55, 57, "Where, O death, is your victory? Where, O death, is your sting?... But thanks be to God! He gives us the victory through our Lord Jesus Christ."

- Genesis 2:7, "Then the Lord God formed a man from the dust of the ground and breathed into his nostrils the breath of life, and the man became a living being."

- "Neither death nor life can break me"
  - Concept: reflecting the unbreakable love of God and His protection
  - Scripture Reference:
    - Romans 8:38–39, "For I am convinced that neither death nor life, neither angels nor demons, neither the present nor the future, nor any powers will be able to separate us from the love of God that is in Christ Jesus our Lord."

- "Lead me to be a leader, teach me to be a teacher"
  - Concept: a plea for spiritual growth and guidance
  - Scripture References:
    - Psalm 25:4–5, "Show me your ways, Lord, teach me your paths. Guide me in your truth and teach me, for you are God my Savior."
    - James 3:1, "Not many of you should become teachers, my fellow believers, because you know that we who teach will be judged more strictly."

- "God is good, all the time. All the time, God is good"
  - Concept: the eternal goodness of God
  - Scripture Reference:
    - Psalm 145:9, "The Lord is good to all; he has compassion on all he has made."
    - Psalm 136:1, "Give thanks to the Lord, for he is good. His love endures forever."

- "Walk by faith"
  - Concept: living by faith, not by sight
  - Scripture Reference:
    - 2 Corinthians 5:7, "For we walk by faith, not by sight."

- "You're my shepherd"
  - Concept: the Lord as our Shepherd

- Scripture Reference:
  - Psalm 23:1, "The Lord is my shepherd; I shall not want" (ESV).

- "Free me from worldly tethers"
  - Concept: the call to focus on Christ and not on earthly things
  - Scripture Reference:
    - Colossians 3:2, "Set your minds on things above, not on earthly things."

- "He is living water"
  - Concept: Jesus as the living water
  - Scripture Reference:
    - John 4:14, "But whoever drinks the water I give them will never thirst. Indeed, the water I give them will become in them a spring of water welling up to eternal life."

- "Fill with desire, Spirit's on fire"
  - Concept: being filled with the Holy Spirit
  - Scripture Reference:
      Acts 2:3–4, "They saw what seemed to be tongues of fire that separated and came to rest on each of them. All of them were filled with the Holy Spirit."

- "Power of prayer, shows you care"
  - Concept: the power of prayer and God's attentiveness
  - Scripture References:
    - James 5:16, "The prayer of a righteous person is powerful and effective."
    - 1 Peter 5:7, "Cast all your anxiety on him because he cares for you."

- "King of earth and of heaven"
  - Concept: Christ's authority over heaven and earth
  - Scripture Reference:
    - Matthew 28:18, "Then Jesus came to them and said, 'All authority in heaven and on earth has been given to me.'"

- "Your love is unbreakable"
  - Concept: the unfailing love of God
  - Scripture Reference:
    - Romans 8:39, "[N]either height nor depth, nor anything else in all creation, will be able to separate us from the love of God that is in Christ Jesus our Lord."

Life We Built Together

[Chorus]
You're my one, you're my only
You're the one, you're the one that I treasure
You're my comfort, you're my best friend
Every day in this life we built together
You're my one, you're my only
You're the one, you're the one that I treasure
You're my comfort, you're my best friend
Every day in this life we built together

Modern Psalms, Volume 1

To the woman I love, the one I call my wife (I love)
Every memory of you fills me with so much pride (I'm proud)
They say every great man has a great woman behind
But everything we've been through,
You've been by my side (you're there)

You know I love you, you know that I cherish you
But what you don't know is just how long that I prayed for you
(I prayed for you)
You leave me speechless, sometimes I don't know what to say to you
The one constant in my life is that I always want to stay with you (stay)
Our vows said till death do us part
And to that point I always thought marriage would be hard (it isn't)
But it's easy when I see you left feeling charmed
And when I'm lost you hold my hand and pull me out the dark

[Chorus]

You support me in everything I do (I do)
So, allow me to take the time to say that I believe in you (I believe in you)
You're the foundation of our family, that's the truth
We've grown together daily since the day we said I do (I do)

At times, the odds been stacked against us
But I'll never give up, as God is my witness
I'm so thankful for the children that you gave me
We built a beautiful family, wow it's so amazing (amazing)

Every morning, you're by my side
And you end every day with a sweet kiss goodnight
I fall more in love when I look into your eyes
And I promise that I'll love you for the rest of my life (I promise)

[Chorus]

Behind the Song

"LIFE WE BUILT TOGETHER" IS DEDICATED to my wife. I remember when I started this music ministry journey and told her about the calling I felt from God. She looked at me like I was crazy—and understandably so. Throughout our marriage, I've started so many passion projects. It's almost like I have a touch of ADHD. Oftentimes, I'd try something new, stick with it for a while, then quit and move on to the next project.

But when I came to my wife and told her I felt like this was a genuine calling, she accepted it gracefully. She had no idea how far it would go, but she supported me, nonetheless. I know that she and I are one flesh, but I can honestly say that she is my better half. I love my wife beyond words; she is truly my best friend. We've been married for ten years now, and we've faced so many hardships together—things that I've seen destroy other marriages. Yet, through it all, she has remained faithful, believing in me and supporting me.

Every day I look at her and think, "I couldn't possibly love her more than I do right now," but every day I'm proven wrong. She looks to me to lead our family and trusts my decisions completely. On days when I struggle with self-doubt or battle depression, she becomes my comfort. I had prayed for a woman like her my entire life. It seems like in every previous relationship, I was unknowingly trying to mold each girlfriend into the woman my wife would be.

Praise God for unanswered prayers, because so many times I thought I was in love, but I learned that I was only in love with the idea of being in love. Before we got married, I'd always heard people say marriage is hard, but that hasn't been my experience at all. Marriage has been incredibly easy for me—natural and not forced. We've been through tough times, but we've always been on the same side, relying on each other until the storm passed.

In this song, I say that my wife is the foundation of our family, and that's an understatement. She is the strongest woman I know, capable of bearing so much. She truly is the glue that holds our family together. With this song, I wanted to acknowledge how much I appreciate her support in everything I do. But I also wanted to send her a message that I believe in her as well. I know the words in this song don't fully match her actions, but I hope it shows how much she means to me.

To the listener and reader, I'd like to share some wisdom I've gleaned from my journey in marriage. A foundational aspect of understanding love is found in 1 Corinthians 13:4-7, which provides a powerful and timeless definition of true love:

> *"Love is patient, love is kind. It does not envy, it does not boast, it is not proud. It does not dishonor others, it is not self-seeking, it is not easily angered, it keeps no record of wrongs. Love does not delight in evil but rejoices with the truth. It always protects, always trusts, always hopes, always perseveres."*

This Bible passage is often recited at weddings, so much so that some may perceive it as cliché. However, the reality is that many who hear these words may not truly live by them. It's essential to recognize that love is not just an emotion; it is an active choice and a daily commitment to embody these qualities.

In our marriage, my wife and I abide by three principles that help keep our relationship strong. The first principle we adhere to is that God is the foundation of our relationship. Whenever we face disagreements or challenges, we turn to the Bible as our common ground—an unbiased source of truth that helps us navigate conflict. This shared belief acts as a guiding light in our relationship, allowing us to say, "Let both of us be liars, but this Word is truth." Without such a foundation, it becomes too easy for misunderstandings to build walls between us, turning minor disagreements into major arguments.

Our second principle is the importance of being willing to apologize. Many conflicts could be averted with a simple, sincere "I'm sorry." This two-word phrase holds incredible power to disarm tension and initiate healing. When we commit to addressing issues before they escalate, we create an environment of openness and vulnerability. Apologizing doesn't signify weakness; instead, it shows strength in recognizing our mistakes and valuing our relationship above our pride.

The third principle revolves around trusting each other wholeheartedly. I know couples who guard their phones with passwords, creating barriers. Such secrecy can breed insecurity and doubt, leading to unnecessary strain in the relationship. Instead, when one spouse expresses insecurity, the other should respond with compassion, taking the time to reassure them. This might mean allowing access to each other's phones or social media accounts, which will foster transparency. By addressing insecurities head-on and showing that there's nothing to fear, we can transform potential conflict into an opportunity for deeper connection and trust.

With these three foundational principles—establishing God as the center, practicing sincere apologies, and cultivating trust—I genuinely believe any marriage can withstand life's storms. God desires for our marriages to thrive, and I believe He grieves when vows are broken. This statement isn't a judgment but rather an acknowledgment of the sanctity of the marital covenant.

When we approach marriage with the same dedication that we give our relationship with Jesus Christ, we set ourselves up for success. Just as being a follower of Christ requires us to die to ourselves and live for Him, marriage demands that we prioritize our spouse over our own desires and entitlement. In doing so, true love can flourish and reach greater heights.

Ultimately, I believe that marriage teaches us how to love Christ more deeply. As we learn to put our spouse's needs above our own, we prepare ourselves for the eternal relationship we will have with our Savior, recognizing that we are His bride. This preparation calls us to embody the qualities of love described in 1 Corinthians 13, shaping our hearts for the day we will live eternally in His presence.

Through the lessons of marriage, we can cultivate a love that mirrors Christ's—sacrificial, unwavering, and transformative. In this way, our earthly relationships become a beautiful reflection of our heavenly calling.

Though there's not much Scripture in this song, the message is rooted in biblical values. Here are some Scriptures that align with what I was trying to express:

- "To the woman I love, the one I call my wife"
  - Scripture Reference:
    - Ephesians 5:25, "Husbands, love your wives, just as Christ loved the church and gave himself up for her."

- "Our vows said till death do us part"
  - Scripture Reference:
    - Mark 10:9, "Therefore what God has joined together, let no one separate."

- "You've been by my side"
  - Scripture Reference:
    - Ecclesiastes 4:9–10, "Two are better than one… If either of them falls down, one can help the other up."

- "You support me in everything I do"
  - Scripture Reference:
    - Proverbs 31:10–12, "A wife of noble character who can find? She is worth far more than rubies. Her husband has full confidence in her and lacks nothing of value. She brings him good, not harm, all the days of her life."

- "We've grown together daily since the day we said 'I do'"
  - Scripture Reference:
    - Ephesians 4:2–3, "Be completely humble and gentle; be patient, bearing with one another in love. Make every effort to keep the unity of the Spirit through the bond of peace."

- "At times, the odds have been stacked against us"
  - Scripture Reference:
    - Romans 8:28, "And we know that in all things God works for the good of those who love him, who have been called according to his purpose."

- "I'm so thankful for the children you gave me"
  - Scripture Reference:
    - Psalm 127:3, "Children are a heritage from the Lord, offspring a reward from him."

- "I fall more in love when I look into your eyes"
  - Scripture Reference:
    - Song of Solomon 4:9, "You have stolen my heart, my sister, my bride; you have stolen my heart with one glance of your eyes."

Follow Me

[Chorus]
Narrow are the gates, but you can make it if you follow Me
Faith the size of a mustard seed, I'll provide all you need
You can choose to follow the world, or you can follow Me
Pick up your cross and follow Me!
Pick up your cross and follow Me!
Follow Me! Follow Me! Yeah, follow Me!
Walk on water! Walk on water!
Pick up your cross and follow Me!
Follow Me! Follow Me! Yeah, follow Me!
Walk on water! Walk on water!

Modern Psalms, Volume 1

Pick up your cross and follow Me!

Spending your time on Facebook, too afraid to face the Book
But it's TikTok till Christ returns
Reflect on that selfie, how's it look
If you live for acceptance, you die from rejection
You want to see power — resurrection
The unworthy are worthy, that's the lesson
You can't live in this world and in death see heaven
Jesus Christ is that tomb raider
There's nothing greater when it comes to the Savior
He's the breaker of the undertaker
To erase the sins of our sinful nature
You felt alone like nobody cared
The world's got you spiritually impaired
You don't have to feel exposed and bared
Just open your eyes and Jesus is there

[Bridge]
If God is for us, who can be against us?
There is no fear in love, witness His forgiveness
Pick up your cross and follow Me!

[Chorus]

Living your life on autopilot, blind to the King like Pontius Pilate
Hiding away your true self in private
Let me show you who Jesus Christ is
He's always there from the womb to the tomb
The Holy Spirit sees what you consume
From your social media to the modern news
Even the secrets locked in your room
But take His hand, he'll show you freedom
Let your bond to the world be weakened
Value faith more than human reason
All He asks is you admit you need Him
Break away the chains from Satan
Rescue you from mental mayhem Stand with you through all your facing
Even the wind and the waters obey Him (church)

[Bridge]

[Chorus]

Behind the Song

"FOLLOW ME" WAS A UNIQUE and interesting song to write. I wanted to point out the flaws we have as people and why we often struggle with faith, but I also wanted to do it in a fun and engaging way. The lyrics reflect what was weighing heavily on my heart at the time: following the narrow road that leads to heaven.

I think the instrumental track is heavy yet exciting, perfectly complementing the message I wanted to communicate. That's the essence of Christian hip hop—music that's fresh and modern, but without the sinfulness found in secular music. It's about glorifying Christ, teaching about Scripture, and spreading the Gospel in a way that truly resonates with listeners. Music is such a powerful tool for reaching people, and even God Himself loves it. It's a great way to honor and glorify Him.

In Scripture, Jesus calls us to pick up our cross and follow Him, but you have to ask yourself: what is my cross? It often involves getting rid of a false idol—something that can take many forms: social media, your phone, lustful images, video games, television, or even self-worship.

It's both sobering and troubling when Christians spend hours on social media but then say they can't find time to read the Bible. We live in a society constantly seeking acceptance, but this goal can never truly be fully achieved. The pursuit itself becomes a distraction, because it has no end. If you live only for acceptance, you'll die from rejection. Christians are called to be in the world but not of the world. A person who never resists sin will struggle to reflect Christ.

One of the most amazing gifts Jesus Christ gave us is immortality. Jesus defeated death, and because of Him, death has lost its sting—it's no longer something we should fear. Society, however, is structured to make us fit in, but the truth is that the desire to do so often leaves us feeling more alone.

When you scroll through social media, you only see a façade—the vacations, the influencers glamorized by makeup and lighting. You don't see their real struggles and insecurities. Jesus Christ is the opposite. In Him, we are never alone. In my experience, I've never felt abandoned or without His presence. Especially when reading the Bible—He speaks to me, encouraging me in my daily life and struggles.

When Jesus ascended into heaven, He sent the Holy Spirit to be with us. Too often, we forget that the Holy Spirit lives within us—seeing everything we see, hearing everything we hear, and feeling everything we feel. When you recognize this, you have a choice: do you want the Holy Spirit to rejoice over your actions and guide your walk of faith, or do you want Him to be grieved by the evil you allow into your life? On the Day of Judgment, Jesus will be our Intercessor, but the Holy Spirit will be a Witness. What will the Spirit say about you?

The only thing Jesus asks of us is to have faith in Him. I'm reminded of Peter's faith, which enabled him to step out of the boat and walk on water. Jesus wasn't the only one who walked on water—He demonstrated that if we have faith in Him, we have the ability to do the impossible. Even in the midst of a storm, Peter trusted Jesus enough to walk on water towards Him.

Do you have that kind of faith? If not, how do we get there?

Jesus and the Holy Spirit are with us from the womb until our last breath. Remind yourself daily of His power. How powerful is He, you ask? Even the wind and the waters obey Him! That's the God we have access to.

If we keep our eyes and faith on Him, we can shed the worldly burdens that distract us. It's like eating candy your whole life and then God offers you nourishing broccoli. Satan tempts us with what our flesh desires, but it leaves us broken and empty. Christ offers living water—His presence, salvation, and eternity. These are free gifts, available if we simply pick up our cross and follow Him.

In the Beginning

These are the Scriptures that I had in mind while writing "Follow Me":

- "Narrow are the gates, but you can make it if you follow Me"
    - Scripture Reference:
        - Matthew 7:13–14, "Enter through the narrow gate. For wide is the gate and broad is the road that leads to destruction, and many enter through it. But small is the gate and narrow the road that leads to life, and only a few find it."

- "Faith the size of a mustard seed, I'll provide all you need"
    - Scripture Reference:
        - Matthew 17:20, "Truly I tell you, if you have faith as small as a mustard seed, you can say to this mountain, 'Move from here to there,' and it will move. Nothing will be impossible for you."

- "Pick up your cross and follow me!"
    - Scripture Reference:
        - Matthew 16:24, "Then Jesus said to his disciples, 'Whoever wants to be my disciple must deny themselves and take up their cross and follow me.'"

- "Walk on water!"
    - Scripture Reference:
        - Matthew 14:29, "Then Peter got down out of the boat, walked on the water and came toward Jesus."

- "If God is for us, who can be against us?"
    - Scripture Reference:
        - Romans 8:31, "What, then, shall we say in response to these things? If God is for us, who can be against us?"

- "There is no fear in love"
    - Scripture Reference:
        - 1 John 4:18, "There is no fear in love. But perfect love drives out fear, because fear has to do with punishment. The one who fears is not made perfect in love."

- "Even the wind and the waters obey him"
  - Scripture Reference:
    - Matthew 8:27, "The men were amazed and asked, 'What kind of man is this? Even the winds and the waves obey him!'"

God Moment

I literally melted down to the floor with my face into the chair
I had no more words to pray anymore,
I had no tears to cry, I was just numb and silent
And in that very moment,
I felt so vividly like Jesus himself
Was standing by the doors of my heart

[Chorus]
We all have our testimony that we share

Modern Psalms, Volume 1

It leads to the second that we know that You're there
We make ourselves our greatest opponent
He rescues us and that's our God, that's our God moment
I was blind, but now I see
How much that I needed You
And how much that You mean to me
I'm witnessing everything
That Your glory and blessings bring
I'm just a human being
And You will always be my King
I don't know what my purpose
On earth is, I'm worthless
I'm doubtful and I'm nervous
Even while writing verses
But You told me to reverse this
I'm worthy of Your purchase
My burdens won't surface
While I'm in Your service
My salvation can't be stolen
All because the Son's a-rosen
Let Your words through me be spoken
Shake the world with an explosion
Your spirit's no longer dormant
I'm hopeful and my heart is open
Praise God, I'm one of the chosen
All because of the God moment

[Chorus]

You saved me, You really saved me
I was dead and You raised me
I find it so amazing
You could have erased me
Instead You embraced me
The fraud I was portraying
Needed Your replacing
I don't know what You see in me
It's defeating me
I welcome the peace it brings

In the Beginning

From choking to breathing
You're my lifesaver
Now I'm highly favored
You got me loving neighbors
I'm embracing in this labor
So shape me, mold me
I need You to hold me
Pick me up, console me
I'm not used to seeing holy
I need less of me, I need more of You
You gave me a mission, and I guarantee to see it through

[Chorus x2]

Behind the Song

"**G**OD MOMENT" IS A SONG I BELIEVE everyone can relate to. The concept came to me while attending a local Bible study, led by my brother-in-Christ, Grant. Every week, Grant would ask us if we had experienced any "God moments"—those experiences or events that we knew could only be from God. I loved the phrase "God moment" and reflected on it for weeks. I realized that every believer has these moments, and our testimonies, as powerful as they are, often trace back to our *original* God moment.

I wanted the song to sound beautiful because all of our God moments are beautiful. But I faced a familiar challenge as before: I couldn't sing. While developing the song's concept, a Christian singer named Olga Gavrilov commented on one of my videos, saying she liked my music. Being a new artist, this stood out to me. I visited her profile and listened to a few of her songs, and I was speechless. Her voice has a beauty and innocence to it that feels irreplaceable. Honestly, I believe she could win something like *America's Got Talent* or *American Idol* if she were to audition.

Amazed that someone with such talent liked my music, I messaged Olga immediately and asked if she would like to collaborate on this song. To my delight, she agreed. I wrote the lyrics and sent her the chorus to sing. During this process, she sent me an audio file of her testimony. You could hear raindrops in the background, and the shakiness in her voice as she spoke made it clear how vulnerable and authentic she was at that moment. Initially, she didn't want me to use it in the song, but I pleaded with her, explaining the vision I had for it. Once everything was recorded and brought together, it was perfect. And that's how "God Moment" came to be!

The song opens with the statement, "I was blind, but now I see," echoing the timeless words of the hymn "Amazing Grace." This phrase resonates deeply with Christians because it encapsulates the profound and transformative reality of what it means to come to faith. In these opening lines, I recount the moment when I first truly witnessed the fullness of salvation—the beauty, blessings, love, and knowledge that accompany it. This revelation was overwhelming, leaving me in awe of the grace I had received. Amidst this overwhelming joy, a small voice in the back of my mind kept asking, "Do I deserve this?"

Before I found Christ, my life was riddled with struggles. I battled low self-esteem and carried heavy burdens of insecurity that often left me feeling trapped in darkness. There were even moments when self-harm crossed my mind, and I genuinely believed that the world would be better off without me. These thoughts were a reflection of the depths of my brokenness. Yet, despite all my flaws and failures, Christ saw something in me worth saving. He rebuilt me from the inside out, transforming my life in ways I never thought possible. Even today, I find myself questioning, "Did He really save me?" It's a humbling realization that I was once lost, consumed by sin, and it would have been justified for God to erase me from existence. But instead, He chose to embrace me with open arms, offering me love and redemption. I still struggle to understand what He sees in me, but I'm eternally grateful that He sees something worth loving.

This experience of salvation reminds me of military boot camp—a concept I have come to understand through friends who have served. They describe it as a rigorous process where individuals are intentionally broken down, only to be rebuilt with a renewed sense of purpose. Through this transformation, they learn to think beyond themselves and dedicate their lives to serving a greater cause. That's the closest analogy I can find for what salvation feels like—an intense and beautiful reconstruction of the self. Just as soldiers emerge from boot camp transformed, I emerged from my encounter with Christ renewed and with a sense of mission.

Even now, as I continue my journey of faith, I approach it with a humble mentality. Many Christians encourage one another to "pray with expectation," yet I often find myself feeling unworthy of asking for anything more. God has already bestowed upon me the greatest gift of all—salvation. Everything else in my life—my home, my family, and my daily blessings—are gifts I don't deserve but humbly receive with deep gratitude, recognizing them as expressions of His divine grace. This perspective shifts my focus from entitlement to appreciation, reminding me to cherish each one.

Through the song lyrics, I reach out to God, asking Him to console me because I'm still not accustomed to seeing the holy in my life. The magnitude of what Christ has shown me through His sacrifice often feels beyond my understanding, filling me with wonder and reverence. As I conclude the song with the plea, "I need less of me, I need more of you," I remind myself of the ongoing battle between my flesh and my spirit. While my flesh still craves the temporary pleasures of this world, my soul—empowered by the Holy Spirit—longs for deeper intimacy with God.

I pray that, if you haven't already, you will find your own God moment, an experience that opens your eyes to the reality of His love and grace for you. May you encounter the transformative power of salvation that I have experienced, leading you to a life marked by gratitude, humility, and a yearning for more of Him.

Scriptures I reflected on while writing "God Moment":

- "I was blind, but now I see"
  - Concept: the man healed by Jesus
  - Scripture Reference:
    - John 9:25, "One thing I do know. I was blind but now I see!"
    - It's also famously echoed in the hymn "Amazing Grace."

Modern Psalms, Volume 1

- "My salvation can't be stolen, All because the Son's a-rosen"
  - Concept: the assurance of salvation through Christ's resurrection
  - Scripture References:
    - John 10:28–29, "I give them eternal life, and they shall never perish; no one will snatch them out of my hand. My Father, who has given them to me, is greater than all; no one can snatch them out of my Father's hand."
    - 1 Corinthians 15:20, "But Christ has indeed been raised from the dead, the firstfruits of those who have fallen asleep."

- "You saved me, You really saved me. I was dead and You raised me"
  - Concept: spiritual rebirth and being made alive in Christ
  - Scripture Reference:
    - Ephesians 2:4–5, "But because of his great love for us, God, who is rich in mercy, made us alive with Christ even when we were dead in transgressions—it is by grace you have been saved."

- "I'm just a human being, And You will always be my King"
  - Concept: a reflection of human frailty and Christ's kingship
  - References:
    - Psalm 8:4, "What is mankind that you are mindful of them, human beings that you care for them?"
    - Revelation 17:14, "They will wage war against the Lamb, but the Lamb will triumph over them because he is Lord of lords and King of kings—and with him will be his called, chosen and faithful followers."

- "I'm hopeful and my heart is open, Praise God, I'm one of the chosen"
  - Concept: this reflects God's calling for believers
  - Scripture Reference:
    - Ephesians 1:4–5, "For he chose us in him before the creation of the world to be holy and blameless in his sight. In love, he predestined us for adoption to sonship through Jesus Christ."

- "You gave me a mission, and I guarantee to see it through"
    - Concept: believers have been given a mission in Christ (the Great Commission)
    - Scripture Reference:
        - Matthew 28:19–20, "Therefore go and make disciples of all nations… And surely I am with you always, to the very end of the age."

Love of a Father

(Father) I love you, Son
(Son) I love you, Daddy
(Father) You're my best friend
(Son) You're my best friend
(Father) I love you
(Son) I love you
(Father) I love you
(Son) I love you
(Father) Forever and ever

(Son) Ever and ever
(Father) Amen
(Son) Amen
[Chorus]
You're the flesh of my flesh
The blood of my blood
Time changes many things
But it'll never change my love
I pray you know your worth
I'll never cause you hurt
You hold the keys to my heart
You've had them since birth
My son you are my legacy
I'll always love you jealously
No matter what your destiny
One thing is always guaranteed
It's been this way since Genesis, since time has first begun
No love is more sacred than a father and a son.

From the moment I saw you I knew that you were mine
I felt like I couldn't breathe until I heard you cry
I never knew that I was blind
Until I looked into your eyes
My love for my wife
Was laying there alive

My son, you are a piece of me
That brings peace to me
I fell in love immediately
As I watched you sleeping peacefully
It's my job to love you
It's my job to teach you
If life causes you to stumble
I'll open my arms and reach you
I'll wipe away your tears
I'll chase away your fears
I'll teach you to be fierce
Yet patient and sincere
It's been this way since Genesis, since time has first begun

In the Beginning

No love is more sacred than a father and a son.

[Chorus]
Everyday you're getting older and I'm watching you grow
From walking to talking, I'm wishing time would slow
I love you, Son, much more than you'll ever know
Every time you smile at me my feelings overflow

Let me give you guidance
There's wisdom found in silence
Face the world with defiance
Learn to do it without violence
Get your knowledge from the Bible
Every Gospel is vital
It'll keep you stable so you don't spiral
It's the key to your soul's survival

Your daddy follows Christ
I trust Him with my life
I pray that you follow me
That's our Creator's design
It's been this way since Genesis, since time has first begun
No love is more sacred than a father and a son

[Chorus x2]

John 17: 22–23
"I have given them the glory that you gave me. That they may be one as we are one—I in them and you in me—so that they may be brought to complete unity. Then the world will know that you sent me and have loved them as you have loved me."

Behind the Song

"LOVE OF A FATHER" IS DEDICATED to my two sons. The moment I received the instrumental from Piero Digilio, I knew exactly what its purpose would be. Writing the lyrics was a fast and effortless process—every feeling I have in my heart and soul for my children poured out effortlessly onto the page.

But before diving into the song, I want to share my personal testimony of becoming a father. When my wife first told me she was pregnant with our first son, I cried—but they weren't tears of joy. They were tears of sorrow. I never wanted children. The idea of becoming a father terrified me. At the time, my wife and I had just lost our home and moved into an apartment in a less-than-ideal part of town. My fears were rooted in practical concerns: my poor health, our unstable finances, and the fact that we weren't living in a safe environment for raising a child. But if I were to be honest, my biggest fear was selfish—I didn't want anything to disrupt my marriage. I had seen so many couples with beautiful relationships become distant after having children, and I didn't want that to happen to us. I called my mom and my best friend, sobbing about these worries.

Throughout my wife's pregnancy, I wore a fake smile during family gatherings and doctor's appointments, concealing my inner turmoil. Even when she went into labor, these thoughts lingered in the back of my mind. But the moment my son was born, everything changed. As I held him and looked into his eyes, every fear and negative thought disappeared. I experienced a love unlike anything I had ever known—a love that filled a void in me I didn't even realize was there.

I'm not ashamed to admit I was completely wrong. My son was the gift my soul had longed for, and I realized that all my fears were unfounded. Instead of causing division between me and my wife, our son united us and transformed our marriage into a family. And now, after the birth of our second son, I feel an even deeper connection—not only with my wife and other son, but also with God, as I witness His faithfulness and love unfolding in our lives.

"Love of a Father" begins with a simple song that my sons and I have shared for as long as I can remember. It's a melody that has woven itself into the fabric of our relationship(s), a cherished tradition that feels timeless.

One poignant line from the song resonates deeply with me: "Time changes many things, but it will never change my love." This is a message I want to instill in my sons, a reminder that my love for them is unwavering and eternal. Having faced the pain of abandonment in my own childhood, I am determined that my children will never feel that void. My role as their father is to be a protective shield, safeguarding them from the negativity and false ideologies that the world may try to impose upon them.

I wrote that my sons hold the keys to my heart, and they've had them since the moment they were born. This love is fiercely loyal and unconditional; nothing they could ever do will alter that bond. It saddens me to witness parents who treat their children as burdens, failing to recognize the miraculous gifts they truly are. Children provide us with a unique lens through which we can see the world anew, with innocence and wonder that reminds us of life's purest joys.

The sacredness of the father-son relationship is a recurring theme throughout Scripture. Even Jesus, in His profound oneness with God, spoke of God the Father with the innocence and overwhelming love characteristic of a Son. This dynamic serves as a blueprint for fatherhood, and it is something I strive to embody with my own boys. I want them to understand that their worth is inherent, grounded in love, and not contingent upon their achievements or failures.

A line in the song states, "I was blind until I looked into his eyes." My sons represent the living manifestation of the love that my wife and I share, and every time I gaze into their eyes, I am reminded of that love's power and beauty. The passion that exists between my wife and me is beautifully reflected in our children—a humbling and awe-inspiring realization that fills my heart with gratitude.

However, fatherhood also comes with its bittersweet moments. Each day, filled with pride, I watch my children grow as they learn to walk, to talk, and to develop their unique personalities. Yet in those moments, I often wish I could slow time down. These fleeting experiences are life's true treasures, far more valuable than any material wealth. And when the days pass so swiftly that I struggle to fully appreciate them, I'm reminded of the importance of being present.

As my children grow, I plan to instill in them the strength to stand firm in their faith, even when it means going against the grain of the world. It's essential that I teach them to remain steadfast in love and nonviolence, as society often promotes aggression as a means to an end—whether through words or actions. If I fail to lead by example, the world will attempt to raise my children according to its own flawed standards.

I want my children to witness every aspect of my faith—reading Scripture, praying, attending Bible studies, sharing the Gospel, kneeling at the altar, and glorifying Jesus Christ in everything I do. Through my actions, they'll come to understand that my relationship with Jesus is authentic and foundational, not merely a routine practiced once a week, or a tradition observed during holidays. My faith is the bedrock of who I am, and it shapes the values I aim to pass down to them.

As the lyrics say, "It's been this way since Genesis, since time has first began. No love is more sacred than a father and a son." This statement encapsulates the sincere connection I share with my sons that is rooted in love, trust, and faith. It's a legacy I hope to nurture in my children, allowing them to thrive in a world that often seeks to diminish the beauty of such relationships. By instilling these values in them, I pray they will carry this sacred bond and the lessons of love into their own lives guiding them as they navigate their own journeys of faith and fatherhood.

Modern Psalms, Volume 1

Several Scriptures were on my heart as I wrote this song:

- Concept throughout:
    - Scripture Reference:
        - John 17:22–23, "I have given them the glory that you gave me, that they may be one as we are one—I in them and you in me—so that they may be brought to complete unity. Then the world will know that you sent me and have loved them even as you have loved me."
    - Context: Jesus's high priestly prayer, expressing unity, love, and shared identity between Father, Son, and believers.
    - Connection: This mirrors the song's theme of deep relational unity, love passed down, and identity rooted in relationship.

- "Flesh of my flesh, blood of my blood"
    - Scripture Reference:
        - Genesis 2:23, "This is now bone of my bones and flesh of my flesh."
    - Context: This verse was originally spoken by Adam about Eve, but biblically establishes covenantal family unity.
    - Connection: I am applying this language to father and son, which fits the biblical idea of lineage and covenant family.

- "It's been this way since Genesis, since time first begun"
    - Scripture Reference: Genesis Chapters 1–2
    - Context: Genesis establishes family, fatherhood, creation order, and generational blessing.
    - Connection: This lyric roots father-son love in God's original design.

- "My son, you are my legacy"
    - Scripture Reference:
        - Psalm 127:3–5, "Children are a heritage from the Lord, offspring a reward from him. Like arrows in the hands of a warrior are children born in one's youth. Blessed is the man whose quiver is full of them."

- "I pray you know your worth"
  - Scripture References:
    - Matthew 10:29–31, "Are not two sparrows sold for a penny? Yet not one of them will fall to the ground outside your Father's care. And even the very hairs of your head are all numbered. So don't be afraid; **you are worth more than many sparrows.**"
    - Psalm 139:13–14, "For you created my inmost being; you knit me together in my mother's womb. **I praise you because I am fearfully and wonderfully made;** your works are wonderful, I know that full well.
  - Comment: Human worth is grounded in God's creation and care.

- "I will open my arms and reach you"
  - Scripture Reference:
    - Luke 15:20 (Parable of the Prodigal Son), "But while he was still a long way off, his father saw him and was filled with compassion… he ran to his son."
  - Comment: This is a strong allusion to the fatherly love of God welcoming a child home.

- "I will wipe away your tears"
  - Scripture Reference:
    - Revelation 21:4, "He will wipe every tear from their eyes."
  - Comment: This line echoes God's promise of comfort, applying it through fatherhood.

- "Teach you to be fierce, yet patient and sincere"
  - Scripture References:
    - Joshua 1:9, "Be strong and courageous. Do not be afraid; do not be discouraged, for the Lord your God will be with you wherever you go."
    - Galatians 5:22–23, "But the fruit of the Spirit is love, joy, peace, forbearance, kindness, goodness, faithfulness, gentleness and self-control."
  - Comment: These lyrics and verses emphasize strength balanced with Christlike character.

- "Get your knowledge from the Bible, every gospel is vital"
  - Scripture References:
    - 2 Timothy 3:16, "All Scripture is God-breathed and useful for teaching."
    - Romans 1:16, "For I am not ashamed of the gospel, because it is the power of God that brings salvation to everyone who believes."
  - Comment: These lyrics and verses show a clear affirmation of Scripture and the Gospel as foundational truth.

- "It's the key to your soul's survival"
  - Scripture References:
    - Matthew 4:4, "Man shall not live on bread alone, but on every word that comes from the mouth of God."
    - John 6:68, "You have the words of eternal life."

- "Your daddy follows Christ"
  - Scripture Reference:
    - 1 Corinthians 11:1, "Follow my example, as I follow the example of Christ."
  - Comment: This verse depicts Paul's model of generational discipleship.

- Father–son love as sacred
  - Scripture Reference:
    - Malachi 4:6, "He will turn the hearts of the fathers to their children, and the hearts of the children to their fathers."
    - Ephesians 6:4, "Fathers, do not exasperate your children; instead, bring them up in the training and instruction of the Lord."

Other verses that reflect the same themes:
- Genesis 18:19, "For I have chosen him, so that he will direct his children and his household after him to keep the way of the Lord by doing what is right and just, so that the Lord will bring about for Abraham what he has promised him."
- Proverbs 22:6, "Start children off on the way they should go, and even when they are old they will not turn from it."
- Proverbs 23:24, "The father of a righteous child has great joy; a man who fathers a wise son rejoices in him."

Witness the Spirit

[Chorus]
Your blood gets to pumping
When you catch the Holy Spirit
This place gets to jumping when
You're filled with the Spirit
He's energetic with no limit
This feeling can't be mimicked
You want it, come and get it
Witness the Holy Spirit!
 (Repeat)

Jesus sent the Spirit of truth
He lives in me, and He lives in you
His energy can fill the room
A burning fire that consumes
To be with us 'til Christ resumes
To guard the bride 'til they see the Groom
When you die to yourself – entombed
Then the Spirit awakens – exhumed
He's the one that Jesus trust
He speaks to the Father on behalf of us
Protects our souls and keeps us just
Until our flesh, it turns to dust
He fills the void of emptiness
Never doubt His sentience
His power's known to be limitless
It's backed by many witnesses

He's your comfort and your advocate
Falling short – inadequate
His blessing's all extravagant
But to dismiss it that's blasphemous
Feel His presence, feel His power
Anticipate this holy encounter
With His strength I'll never cower
He's with me in my darkest hour

[Chorus x2]

Holy spirit wash over me
I offer complete control of me
My body is Your embassy
For Your spiritual diplomacy
Convict me of my sins
Help me to repent
Reveal my true intent
Make me a fisher of men

So, lead me, guide me
I'm so tired of hiding

In the Beginning

From evil that is blinding
It fears that You're inside me
With You I can walk on water
Like I'm stepping to the altar
Witness sons and daughters
That my faith will never falter

Please accept my submission
Show me when to talk and when to listen
Help me to fulfill my mission
To defeat the evil opposition
Your ways may be strange to us
But I know You're someone I can trust
With You living inside of me
My faith has become dangerous

[Chorus x2]

Behind the Song

I WROTE "WITNESS THE SPIRIT" wanting to create an energetic song, and what better topic to choose than the Holy Spirit? It was written with the desire to connect with Pentecostal and charismatic church communities, whose passion for the Holy Spirit I deeply admire. While I am not a member of a Pentecostal church, and don't hold to every doctrinal belief, I respect the fact that they actively seek the Holy Spirit and make Him an integral part of their community. My hope is that this song resonates with that same devotion and offers encouragement to all who long to walk more closely with Him.

One of my primary motivations for writing this song is that the role of the Holy Spirit is not discussed enough in today's church. His mysterious nature, combined with the fact that Scripture contains fewer direct references to Him compared to the Father and the Son, may contribute to this, but it's important for believers to understand who He is.

Throughout the Bible, it's clear that the Holy Spirit is masculine, divine, and an integral part of the Trinity. Jesus, in His wisdom, sent the Holy Spirit to us after His ascension, ensuring that we would not be left alone in our spiritual journey. Since the day of Pentecost (Acts 2:1–3), the Holy Spirit has taken residence within believers, marking a transformative moment in our relationship with God. This indwelling signifies that the Holy of Holies now resides in our hearts, especially since the temple veil was torn, symbolizing that believers now have direct access to God.

On that momentous day of Pentecost, the Holy Spirit manifested as a burning fire, representing both purification and power. Scripture also speaks of a "baptism with the Holy Spirit and fire" (Matthew 3:11; Luke 3:16), a refining work that burns away what is impure and reveals our true selves (Acts 19:2–6).

The Holy Spirit's role is multifaceted: He is our Guide and Guardian, protecting the bride of Christ until we are united with the Groom, Jesus. He intercedes for us, sometimes expressing our unutterable feelings through groans that words cannot convey (Romans 8:26). This deep connection reassures us that we are never alone in our prayers and supplications.

The Holy Spirit holds a unique and vital place within the Godhead. Jesus Himself taught that the only unforgivable sin is blasphemy against Him (Matthew 12:31). The Holy Spirit equips us with spiritual gifts in times of need, empowering us to serve others and fulfill God's purpose for our lives. His presence brings comfort, guidance, and strength—and it's no wonder that evil fears Him. Though much about the Spirit remains a mystery, we can trust Him completely, confident that He is with us in every circumstance.

While Scripture provides detailed descriptions of God the Father and Jesus the Son, the Holy Spirit is less explicitly defined. However, at the moment of salvation, every believer receives His presence within, confirming His faithfulness. This intimate relationship with the Holy Spirit serves as the foundation for our spiritual growth and transformation.

His importance should be emphasized more in our churches, as many people tend to view the Holy Spirit merely as an emotional feeling or experience, overlooking the fact that He is a distinct, divine entity who dwells within us as part of the Trinity. My prayer for listeners and readers is that they actively seek Him and develop a genuine desire to know Him more deeply. Understanding the vital role He plays in our lives, enables us to invite His presence into our conversations, our worship, and our daily lives. By doing so, we can cultivate a richer and deeper faith that embraces the fullness of God's presence through the Holy Spirit.

My goal with this song is to spark a greater conversation about the Holy Spirit, encouraging fellowship among believers that leads to a deeper understanding of His nature and purpose. As we engage in discussions about faith, let us be intentional about including the Holy Spirit in our dialogue, recognizing Him not just as a peripheral presence but as a vital guide in our spiritual journeys. Together, we can grow in understanding, allowing the Holy Spirit to guide us into a deeper relationship with Christ and a more vibrant expression of our faith in the world.

In the Beginning

Here are some Scriptures that were on my heart while writing this song:

- "He's your comfort and your advocate"
    - Concept: Holy Spirit as Advocate and Guide
    - Scripture Reference:
        - John 14:16, "And I will ask the Father, and He will give you another advocate to help you and be with you forever—the Spirit of truth."

- "Feel His presence, feel His power"
    - Concept: Holy Spirit's power and presence
    - Scripture Reference:
        - Acts 1:8, "But you will receive power when the Holy Spirit comes on you; and you will be my witnesses in Jerusalem, and in all Judea and Samaria, and to the ends of the earth."

- "So lead me, guide me"
    - Concept: The Holy Spirit filling and leading
    - Scripture Reference:
        - Romans 8:14, "For those who are led by the Spirit of God are the children of God."

- "My body is your embassy"
    - Concept: believers as the temple of the Holy Spirit
    - Scripture Reference:
        - 1 Corinthians 6:19, "Do you not know that your bodies are temples of the Holy Spirit, who is in you, whom you have received from God? You are not your own."

- "When you die to yourself – entombed / Then the Spirit awakens – exhumed"
    - Concept: dying to self and rising with Christ
    - Scripture Reference:
        - Romans 6:4, "We were therefore buried with Him through baptism into death in order that, just as Christ was raised from the dead through the glory of the Father, we too may live a new life."

- "To dismiss them is blasphemous"
  - Concept: blasphemy against the Holy Spirit
  - Scripture Reference:
    - Matthew 12:31, "And so I tell you, every kind of sin and slander can be forgiven, but blasphemy against the Spirit will not be forgiven."

- "Convict me of my sins"
  - Concept: the Holy Spirit convicting of sin
    - Scripture Reference:
      John 16:8, "When He comes, He will prove the world to be in the wrong about sin and righteousness and judgment."

Take Me as I Am

(Here I am Lord, take me as I am,
Take me as I am, take me as I am)

[Chorus]
Here I am Lord, take me as I am,
Take me as I am Lord take me by the hands
Here I am Lord, take me as I am,
Take me as I am Lord I am but a man (a man)
Here I am Lord, take me as I am,

Take me as I am Lord keep me in Your plans (Your plans)
Here I am Lord, take me as I am,
Take me as I am Lord to the promised land

I can feel You near me, God, I see You clearly
I know You can hear me when my soul is weary
You make my burdens easy; Your yoke is so light
When I find myself in darkness, You pull me towards the light

Failure is so humbling, to accept You I have to know I failed
There are no words to describe, when I came to You the grace I felt
My confidence to prevail, when Your kingdom was unveiled.
You're the air in my lungs, blood in my veins, this isn't a fairy tale
I have the faith of the centurion, God, I already know You won
Your 'Spirit's all around me, accessible to anyone
Let these truths leave my tongue, until I see Your glory come
This world is no substitute, cause light bulbs can't replace the sun

[Chorus]

Glory goes to Jesus, You're the one that freed us
Our actions were all grievous, and still You redeemed us
Made me a believer, rebuked the deceiver
Thirsting for Your knowledge, You became my teacher

I submit my life to His will, the God of Israel, Is real
Everything that prophets revealed
Through Jesus Christ has been fulfilled
So much freedom in being saved, You lifted me out the dirty grave
Walking towards the last days, I've no reason to be afraid
Don't be content in being condemned, neglecting the truth to live in sin
Christ is holding out His hand, asking for you to believe in Him
Eternal life is evident; you determine where it's spent
You can go to church and say you're saved,
But who are you when the service ends

[Chorus]

Here I am Lord, take me as I am, take me as I am, Lord, take me as I am

(Repeat 2x)

Behind the Song

"TAKE ME AS I AM" WAS THE FIRST song I recorded in my home studio. Before that, I always used studios near me, but there were always complications. After taking Rob Ruff's advice, I invested in myself. I bought a recording program, a microphone, and an interface. This was the best investment I've made because now I have the freedom to record anytime I want—with no more studio fees.

The instrumental for this track was made by Piero Digilio, and when I heard the beat, I fell in love with it—it's powerful and emotional. This was also the first time my music was completely produced, mixed, and mastered in-house by Piero Digilio. I'm grateful for his excellent work ethic and kind soul. Many times, he's gone above and beyond for me because he believes in what I'm doing. It's a wonderful feeling to know your producer is in your corner, believing in you, not just in your pockets.

While recording this song, I found that I could almost carry a tune, which was ironic because I had COVID at the time. Whether it was the rasp in my voice or the home studio setup, the recording turned out beautifully.

The core theme behind the song is being bare and exposed before God. We don't have to fix ourselves before seeking Him. Many believe in God but don't pursue a relationship with Him because they feel unworthy. But humanity has been flawed since birth, and we need to realize that God is wiser and stronger than we are. He's the ultimate physician, able to heal and repair every flaw.

The song opens with the words "Here I Am," which are more than just lyrics—they're a powerful declaration of submission to God. I frequently begin my prayers with, "Father, here I am." In doing so, I acknowledge my presence before Him and fully commit my heart and mind to His divine care. This simple phrase serves as a reminder of His might and grace, assuring me that He hears my weary cries. If He can lift my burdens and provide comfort, I am confident that He can do the same for you.

We often make ourselves weary by trying to carry our burdens alone, forgetting that Christ invites us to lay them at His feet. He reassures us that His yoke is easy and His burden is light (Matthew 11:30). This truth serves as a humbling reminder that failure is not the end but a step toward grace. To truly embrace salvation, we must first acknowledge our shortcomings and admit that we haven't fully surrendered to Him. This is what sets Christianity apart from other faiths: we don't have to be perfect to come to Christ. Instead, He invites us to seek Him just as we are, trusting that He will bring about transformation within us.

One of my favorite Bible stories is about the centurion—a Roman officer who, despite not being a Jew, recognized Jesus's power in a way that surpassed the comprehension of many who followed Him. His faith was remarkable: instead of demanding that Jesus come to him, he humbly approached Christ, acknowledging His authority. In a culture where Romans often looked down on Jews, the centurion broke through those societal barriers, believing that Jesus could heal his servant with just a word. This powerful lesson encourages us to deny our natural inclinations toward pride and instead seek a faith that transcends social norms and embraces true humility.

As I conclude the first verse with the line, "Light bulbs can't replace the sun," I emphasize the truth that nothing in this world can compare to the love of Christ. He is the true light that illuminates our lives, and there is no substitute for His transformative presence. In a world filled with distractions and counterfeits, we must remember that the light of Christ is unparalleled and irreplaceable.

I encourage listeners to contemplate whether there has ever been a greater teacher than Jesus. His teachings were not only profound and life changing in His time but continue to resonate powerfully today. The Sermon on the Mount (Matthew 5–7) laid the foundation for many of the moral principles Christians strive to live by. If you haven't read it, I encourage you to dive into its pages. If you have, I invite you to revisit it with fresh eyes, allowing His words to challenge and inspire you anew.

The final verse of the song concludes with two poignant lines. The first, "Don't be content being condemned," resonates deeply, echoing

Jesus's words: "If your eye causes you to sin, pluck it out" (Matthew 5:29). This verse compels us to be proactive in eliminating sin from our lives, whether it involves distancing ourselves from lustful images, certain movies, or music that pulls us away from our walk with God, we are called to take intentional steps toward purity and righteousness.

The second line, "Who are you when the service ends?" invites a moment of reflection: Who are we when we step outside the church? Are we living in a manner that reveals Christ to others? Are we embodying His light in a world so often shrouded in darkness? It challenges us to assess whether our actions and attitudes align with the teachings of Jesus—not just within the walls of the church but in our daily lives. As we go about our week, may we strive to be representatives of Christ, shining His light and love in every interaction, serving as a testament to His transforming power.

In essence, this song calls us to a deeper understanding of our relationship with Christ, urging us to embrace submission to Him, recognizing our need for His grace, and living out our faith with authenticity. Let us not be content with mere church attendance, but instead engage wholeheartedly in our walk with God, reflecting His love and light to the world around us.

Here are the Scriptures I was reflecting on while writing this song:

- "Here I am, Lord"
  - Concept: This phrase echoes Isaiah's response to God's call
  - Scripture Reference:
    - Isaiah 6:8, "Then I heard the voice of the Lord saying, 'Whom shall I send? And who will go for us?' And I said, 'Here am I. Send me!'"

- "You make my burdens easy; Your yoke is so light"
  - Scripture Reference:
    - Matthew 11:30, "For my yoke is easy and my burden is light."

- "Faith of the centurion"
  - Scripture Reference: Matthew 8:5–13, but especially verse 10
    - Matthew 8:10, "When Jesus heard this, he was amazed and said to those following Him, 'Truly I tell you, I have not found anyone in Israel with such great faith.'"

- "Glory goes to Jesus, you're the one that freed us"
  - Scripture Reference:
    - John 8:36, "So if the Son sets you free, you will be free indeed."

- "Rebuked the deceiver"
  - Scripture Reference:
    - James 4:7, "Submit yourselves, then, to God. Resist the devil, and he will flee from you."

- "I submit my life to His will, the God of Israel, is real"
  - Scripture Reference:
    - Romans 12:1, "Therefore, I urge you, brothers and sisters, in view of God's mercy, to offer your bodies as a living sacrifice, holy and pleasing to God—this is your true and proper worship."

- "Everything that prophets revealed through Jesus Christ has been fulfilled"
  - Scripture Reference:
    - Matthew 5:17, "Do not think that I have come to abolish the Law or the Prophets; I have not come to abolish them but to fulfill them."

- "Walking towards the last days"
  - Scripture Reference:
    - 2 Timothy 3:1, "But mark this: There will be terrible times in the last days."

- "Eternal life is evident, you determine where it's spent"
  - Scripture Reference:
    - John 3:16, "For God so loved the world that he gave his one and only Son, that whoever believes in Him shall not perish but have eternal life."

- "Christ is holding out His hand, asking for you to believe in Him"
  - Scripture Reference:
    - Revelation 3:20, "Here I am! I stand at the door and knock. If anyone hears my voice and opens the door, I will come in and eat with that person, and they with me."

Perfect Timing

In my darkest hour, when all hope was gone
You came to my rescue at such a high cost (that cost was too high)
In my moment of need, you heard my faint cry (You heard me)
Your perfect timing (perfect timing) I can't deny (let's go!)

[Chorus]
God's perfect timing so divine (so divine, so divine)
Every twist and every turn
His plan aligns,
Through valleys low
And mountains high (so high, so high)

His perfect timing, our hearts rely

In the Beginning

God came to me at the perfect time, I was just try'na stay alive
He opened my eyes, I realized that if I ask, he provides
Break me of my independence, end it like I did this sentence
I was serving out my sentence, You paid my debt, I'm forgiven

I knew about the lake of fire, but not your grace and mercy
You're the living water, Jesus, I've been thirsty
I knew I wasn't worthy; I was living worldly
Covered in sin and dirty, my vision was all blurry

But you bathed me, saved me, stopped me from being lazy
I know I'm sounding crazy, but judgment doesn't phase me
No one man can shame me, let me put it plainly
This world can never blame me, 'cause Jesus gave me safety

[Chorus]

Perfect timing (perfect timing)

When I thought I was by myself
You was right there behind me (behind me)
When I got off track and I needed alignment
You gave me an assignment, gave me hands to build monuments

To build and not destroy (destroy)
You brought healing and joy (healing and joy)
I experienced death when I was just a little boy
I watched you build mama up when she couldn't take no more (Mama)

She cried, "Wait for the Lord
And make sure you never leave the house
Without the sword (without the sword)
And armor" (and armor)

And do right by people, there will be karma (karma)
No weapon formed will harm you
Even though the enemy has an arsenal (arsenal)
And he's an arsonist

My God is omniscient, He sees all of this (all of this)
He keeps promises, Satan off premises (off premises)
The land is promised
And right now is perfect timing (perfect timing)

Modern Psalms, Volume 1

If I was to be honest (be honest)
To carry your cross like Christ (like Christ)
For your soul there's a price
Follow the light (follow the light)

[Chorus]

His perfect timing, our hearts rely

His timing is perfect, So perfect

Behind the Song

"PERFECT TIMING" WAS ONE OF THE most challenging songs I've written. It's an incredible song, and the featured artists did a phenomenal job, but I really struggled with writing the chorus. I love the background instrumental—it almost has a Celtic vibe—but the chorus section was so unique that it took a lot of brainstorming to figure out how to write it.

The featured artists on this song are Olga Gavrilov and Babikee. Olga's performance on the chorus was amazing. Her voice has a lilt and melody that's unlike anything I've heard before. I'm so thankful for her patience—especially with this song—because it was a true group effort. Babikee, a childhood friend of mine, is a well-known artist in Atlanta's underground rap scene, and I was deeply honored to have him feature on this song.

After the song was released, I received some pushback from the Christian community because Babikee used the word "karma" in his verse. Some criticized it due to the word's origins in another religion, claiming it was inappropriate. However, instead of focusing on the history of a word, consider the context in which it was used. Praise God that a secular artist took a step toward Christian music! In this case, Babikee used the word "karma" simply to mean "repercussions," nothing more. Sometimes we get so caught up in legalism that we overlook the beauty of a message that glorifies Christ.

The song "Perfect Timing" serves as a powerful reminder of how God's timing transcends our understanding. It emphasizes that His knowledge of our needs during every season of life is incomparable to our own limited perspective. In Matthew 6:26–27, we are reminded of God's provision, *"Look at the birds of the air; they do not sow or reap or store away in barns, and yet your Heavenly Father feeds them. Are you not much more valuable than they? Can any one of you by worrying add a single hour to your life?"* This Scripture reassures us that God cares deeply for His creation, providing even for the smallest of creatures. If He does that, how much more will He care for us—His beloved children?

The essence of the song also highlights the beauty of encountering salvation at precisely the right moment in our lives. When I first began my relationship with God, I was merely coasting through life, preoccupied with the struggle to survive due to my health issues. It wasn't until I broke away from my independent mindset and cried out to Him in desperation that I truly experienced His presence. God hears our cries, and through the pages of Scripture, we come to realize how fleeting this life is, yet we are offered something infinitely greater—eternal life through Jesus Christ.

It's crucial to clarify that God is not a genie in a lamp, ready to grant our every wish. While He may not fulfill all our requests as we envision, He, as a loving Father, provides us with exactly what we need. This distinction is vital—it emphasizes that His love and provision are guided by wisdom and purpose, not merely by our desires.

Reflecting on my upbringing, I remember hearing preachers focus heavily on the concepts of hellfire and brimstone, saying, "If you do this or that, you're going to hell." Looking back, many of these messages felt reminiscent of the Pharisees. While it's important to understand the consequences of denying God, how much greater is it to teach about His grace and mercy? Rather than adopting a legalistic approach that condemns others, we should embrace the call to share the Gospel. Focusing solely on condemnation often leaves people feeling defensive creating barriers that prevent them from experiencing God's love. The Gospel—the Good News—is about the incredible sacrifice Jesus made for us. He paid our debt and bore our sins, allowing us to receive mercy instead of judgment.

I have observed that those who find salvation often do so during the lowest moments of their lives—when they are in the valley and cry out to Jesus for help. By showing non-believers how deeply God loves, cares for, and provides for us, we can create an environment where they can lower their defenses, receive the saving grace of Jesus Christ, and allow God to dismantle strongholds and set them free to live the life He planned for them.

At one point in the song, I sing the line: "Judgment doesn't faze me, for no one man can shame me." This reflects my growing security in my faith and trust in my Creator. I've come to the understanding that judgment from others holds no power over me. Each night, I pray for God to reveal any sins I may have committed unknowingly, allowing me the opportunity to learn and repent. It's important to remember that we should not place our trust in man—so many people are quick to point out flaws in our lives. This is why we turn to Scripture. Through daily reading and prayer, the Holy Spirit convicts us, shining His light on the areas where we need to grow.

At times, we may feel a sense of disconnection from God, but it's vital to remember that He is always with us. God is faithful to keep His promises and will never abandon us. If you find yourself in a season of spiritual dryness or distance, I challenge you to press deeper into prayer and immerse yourself in Scripture. Take a moment to reflect on your life and consider whether God is using any challenges or circumstances to draw you closer to Him. No matter how far off track we may feel, God is always present, ready to guide us back and provide the necessary adjustments. We must cultivate a mindset of trust in His perfect timing—trusting that He knows what is best for us, even when the path ahead seems unclear.

Ultimately, "Perfect Timing" calls us to embrace the mystery of God's timing, reassuring us that His plans are always for our good. By surrendering our timelines and expectations to Him, we can find peace and assurance, knowing that He is orchestrating every detail of our lives according to His divine purpose.

Scriptures reflected on during the writing of this song:

- "In my darkest hour, when all hope was gone
  You came to my rescue at such a high cost
  In my moment of need, You heard my faint cry
  Your perfect timing I can't deny"
    - Scripture Reference:
        - Psalm 18:6, "In my distress I called to the Lord; I cried to my God for help. From His temple He heard my voice; my cry came before Him, into His ears."

- "God's perfect timing, so divine
  Every twist and every turn
  His plans align, through valleys low
  And mountains high
  His perfect timing, our hearts rely"
    - Scripture References:
    - "His plans align"
        - Romans 8:28, "And we know that in all things God works for the good of those who love Him, who have been called according to His purpose."
    - "Through valleys low and mountains high"
        - Psalms 23:4, "Even though I walk through the darkest valley, I will fear no evil, for You are with me; Your rod and Your staff, they comfort me."

- "God came to me at the perfect time, I was just try'na stay alive
  He opened my eyes, I realized that if I ask, He provides"
    - Scripture Reference:
        - Matthew 7:7, "Ask and it will be given to you; seek and you will find; knock and the door will be opened to you."

- "You paid my debt, I'm forgiven"
    - Scripture Reference:
        - Romans 6:23, "For the wages of sin is death, but the gift of God is eternal life in Christ Jesus our Lord."

- "I knew about the lake of fire, but not Your grace and mercy You're the living water, Jesus, I've been thirsty"
    - Scripture References:
    - "Lake of fire"
        - Revelation 20:14, "Then death and Hades were thrown into the lake of fire. The lake of fire is the second death."
    - "You're the living water, Jesus"
        - John 4:14, "But whoever drinks the water I give them will never thirst. Indeed, the water I give them will become in them a spring of water welling up to eternal life."

- "Covered in sin and dirty, my vision was all blurry"
    - Scripture Reference:
        - Isaiah 64:6, "All of us have become like one who is unclean, and all our righteous acts are like filthy rags."

In My Darkest Hour

[Chorus]
You were there, my soul was bare
In my darkest hour, You heard my prayer (my prayer)
When I was no one, You made me someone
In my darkest hour, You heard my prayer

You showed me mercy even though I didn't deserve it (I didn't)
Bottom of the barrel, I know I was far from perfect
I was lost and I was searching

Lord, my heart was hurting when I thought that I was worthless
You made me worthy of Your purchase
But that's the past, I'm looking back
I'm letting go, no tit for tat
My old ways are dead and gone
I promise I'm not looking back
Everything is made anew
Lord, I owe my life to You
No more hiding from the truth
You died for me, so I live for You
I was Saul, but You made me Paul
The road to Damascus was feeling long
I was going to places I just didn't belong
But You were there, through it all
And You saved me before the fall

[Chorus]

Now my life has changed, what to do with it
Lord, I need Your guidance
I'm not used to forgiveness, I'm proud to admit it
You healed me of my sickness
I'll never be religious
Speak the truth as Your witness
All my sins been nailed to the cross
Give praises from the air I breathe
Provide me with a dialogue
I don't want to be a Pharisee
I believe You set me free
Revealed to me by prophecies
All these gifts that I received
Because I gave a bended knee
I owe my life to You
I'm blessed to be in servitude
I was abused and confused
But Your grace is absolute
So what to do with life anew
Spend my time in search of You
My faith in You is resolute

I only want to speak Your truth

[Chorus]

So now it's your turn
Are you stubborn
Tell me, will you stand firm
Or embrace the things that you learned
Do you have your eyes closed
Or open to the Bible
Are you open to revival
And becoming a disciple
Turn away from independence
Christ is here, you know He's present
Search forgiveness and repentance
See the kingdom you inherit
Old you was ignorant
New you is innocent
There isn't a coincidence
Judgment is imminent
Will He judge you
Or will He love you
There's no excuse
He sees what all you're going through
His grace is mercy
Water when you're thirsty
Stop being worldly
And join me on this journey

Behind the Song

"IN MY DARKEST HOUR" IS A SONG about God's presence during the most difficult moments of my life. It is unique for me because the first two verses represent my personal testimony and a conversation I had with God, while the third verse speaks directly to the listener.

I was blessed to collaborate with Songs of the Way, an incredibly talented singer from Australia. This was my first time working with him. When I was searching for a singer to feature on the track, I reached out to Olga Gavrilov, and she recommended him. From the moment I heard his voice, I knew he was perfect for the song. His voice has a matchless quality that can command attention from anyone in the room. I'm truly grateful for his contribution, and I look forward to working with him again.

The instrumental for this song has a soothing Far East-inspired theme, which complements the message beautifully. Piero Digilio, the producer, is a master of versatility. His range is remarkable, and he's unafraid to explore new sounds. This song was a perfect example of his creativity.

In the chorus of this song, I share the profound moment when God heard my heartfelt prayer during the darkest hour of my life. It was a time when I stripped away all pretense, laying my soul bare before Him and crying out in desperation. I emphasize this experience because it is foundational to my testimony and the essence of God's transformative power. In that moment, I felt utterly insignificant—just a nobody, lost in a world that seemed indifferent. Yet, as unfathomable as it still is to me, God saw worth in me, even when I couldn't see it myself.

His grace is not merely a concept; it is a reality that manifests in His mercy toward the undeserving. This gift cannot be earned or purchased; it is freely given. It is crucial to internalize this truth—God's mercy is extended even to those who feel unworthy. The weight of this realization is powerful, highlighting the depth of His love for us. The Creator of the universe, who holds the stars in place, knows my name. That alone brings indescribable joy.

As I reflect on my past, I acknowledge the deep pain and trauma I once carried—pain from abandonment, abuse, and the insidious effects of low self-esteem. These wounds ran deep, shaping my identity for far too long. But I now see the person I once was as someone entirely separate from who I am today; that old self has died. I have been transformed, much like Saul on the road to Damascus, who became Paul. The guilt and trauma that once defined me no longer hold power over my life. In moments of struggle, I remind myself of Christ's sacrifice. If He was willing to endure such suffering for my sake, how could I not strive to live for Him?

When Christ reached down to save me from the depths of despair, I was unfamiliar with the concept of forgiveness. Growing up in an environment where pride and arrogance prevailed, forgiveness was rare—mistakes were weaponized, used to punish rather than heal. Encountering Christ, however, completely changed my understanding of forgiveness. Now, it flows freely; it is a gift that rejuvenates the spirit. As Romans 1:16 beautifully articulates, I am unashamed to proclaim the gospel and testify to all that He has done for me.

In the second verse, I express my commitment to authenticity with the line, "I'll never be religious but speak the truth as Your witness." I refuse to confine myself to any one denomination or doctrine. My identity is rooted in being a follower of Christ, liberated from the shackles of legalism and the pitfalls of a Pharisaical mindset. I acknowledge that my journey of faith is ongoing— there is always more to discover and learn. Each time I delve into Scripture, new revelations emerge, illuminating aspects of truth that had previously eluded me. I believe God reveals these insights to us precisely when we are ready to receive them, guiding our growth according to His perfect timing.

There is wisdom in the saying that if you find yourself as the smartest person in the room, it may be time to seek a new environment. It reminds us of the importance of surrounding ourselves with people who challenge us and encourage our spiritual growth. On this journey, we must remain open to learning and growing, allowing our faith to deepen as we engage with others who share the same commitment to Christ. Together, we can inspire one another and reflect the light of Christ in a world that desperately needs hope.

In several of my songs, I touch on the theme of servitude—a role I truly consider myself blessed to be in. Jesus Christ spent His time on earth serving others, teaching that "the least among you will be first in heaven" (Luke 9:48). How incredible is it that the living God chose to dwell among us, never seeking to rule or live lavishly? Instead, He taught by example, serving others and demonstrating that societal status holds no weight in the Kingdom of Heaven. While some people may view the term "servant" with disdain, servitude is a blessing. Whether we realize it or not, we are all servants; the difference is in whom we choose to serve. Will it be the living God or the world? A servant cannot have two masters.

As I mentioned earlier, in the third verse, I speak directly to the listener. I encourage you to look within and ask yourself: Are you being stubborn? Are you willing to embrace what you've learned? There's a common misconception in Christianity that repentance solely refers to the forgiveness of sins, but its true meaning is a change of mind. We are called to transform our thinking. Throughout our lives, we have been conditioned to think in ways that are self-promoting, self-gratifying, and centered on our own interests. God challenges us to shift our focus to Him, and in doing so, to consider the needs of others as well.

One of the main things I believe that is lacking in modern Christianity is a robust approach to discipleship. Too often, individuals are presented with a simple prayer to recite, and after declaring their faith, they are sent on their way with the assurance of salvation. While that initial step is undoubtedly important, it is only the beginning of a much deeper journey.

Many new believers are not taught about the process of sanctification—the ongoing journey of growing in faith and becoming more like Christ. This path requires intentional guidance and mentorship, helping individuals navigate their spiritual development and deepen their understanding of God's Word. Without this foundation, many are left to face their spiritual battles alone, often feeling lost and unsure of how to apply their faith in everyday life.

Furthermore, true discipleship equips individuals to teach others and share the gospel effectively. By engaging in relationships with mentors and fellow believers, Christians learn to share their faith authentically and practically. This ongoing cycle of teaching and learning is crucial for building a vibrant, healthy Christian community—one that actively seeks to fulfill the Great Commission.

It's essential that we bring discipleship back into focus within our churches and communities. By prioritizing it, we unlock the richness of the Christian faith and experience the transformative power of the Holy Spirit in our lives. Discipleship is not just about personal growth; it also furthers the collective growth of the body of Christ. There is so much in the Kingdom of Heaven that we are meant to inherit, and by nurturing a culture of discipleship, we equip future generations to carry Christ's message into the world.

If you have truly given your life to Christ, it's crucial to grasp the full implications of that decision. When you recognize that God Himself entered our world and became a living sacrifice, you begin to understand the depth of His love and the magnitude of His grace. Jesus willingly laid down His life to atone for our sins, showing that salvation is not something we earn through our own efforts or good deeds. Instead, we are saved by grace through faith—a gift we can receive but never deserve.

This understanding invites us to embrace a transformative reality: the old version of ourselves, with all its flaws and ignorance, has been put to death We no longer need to be defined by our past mistakes or the burdens we once carried. Instead, we are called to approach God with the faith and innocence of a child—an innate trust and openness, that He encourages us to adopt in our relationship with God.

Embracing this childlike faith allows us to fully experience the freedom and renewal found in our relationship with Christ. It means letting go of the weight of our past and stepping into the new identity God has given us. This transformation encourages us to approach life with curiosity, humility, and a genuine eagerness to learn from Him.

As we navigate our faith journey, it's essential to remember that the grace we have received is not just a one-time event but a continual invitation to grow and mature in our relationship with God. When we understand that our old selves have died and we are now new creations in Christ, we open ourselves to a life filled with purpose, hope, and joy. This new identity compels us to live out our faith intentionally and share the love of Christ with others, reflecting the transformative power of His grace in our lives.

The question of whether Christ will judge us or embrace us with love upon His return is a profound one that invites deep introspection. When we consider it, we must confront the sobering truth that no excuse will stand. God sees us fully—every thought, every hurt, every joy, and every regret. He understands the complexities of our humanity, for He walked among us and experienced the full spectrum of emotions and pain that we endure.

During His time on earth, Jesus experienced suffering, betrayal, and loss. He entered into the brokenness of humanity—not as a distant observer, but as one who fully shared in our struggles. Because of this, His love and compassion run deep. He does not approach us with condemnation but with the heart of a healer, seeking to mend what is broken and restore what has been lost.

For those who find themselves in a dark hour—whether due to personal struggles, loss, or overwhelming circumstances—there is an urgent invitation to turn to Christ. Submitting to Christ at salvation is not an act of defeat but one of surrender, acknowledging our need for His strength and guidance. When we reach out to Him, we encounter grace and an unconditional love that transcends all our failures and shortcomings.

Accepting the gift He offers means recognizing that salvation and hope are not rewards for good behavior but are freely given to us through His sacrifice. It is an open invitation to experience His love and allow it to change our hearts and minds. This transformation doesn't mean that life will be free of challenges, but it does provide us with the assurance that we are never alone when facing them.

I want to extend a heartfelt invitation for you to join me on this journey of faith. Together, we can explore the depths of His love, navigate the complexities of life, and encourage one another in our walk with Christ. This journey is not merely about personal growth but also about the support and strength we find in community as we seek to reflect the love of Christ in a world that desperately needs it. By embracing this path, we gain hope, purpose, and the assurance that even in our darkest hours, we are held by the One who knows us intimately and loves us unconditionally.

While writing this song, I reflected on several Scriptures that shaped my lyrics:

- "You showed me mercy even though I didn't deserve it"
  - Scripture Reference:
    - Romans 5:8, "But God demonstrates his own love for us in this: While we were still sinners, Christ died for us."

- "My old ways are dead and gone"
  - Scripture Reference:
    - 2 Corinthians 5:17, "Therefore, if anyone is in Christ, the new creation has come: The old has gone, the new is here!"

- "You died for me, so I live for you"
  - Scripture Reference:
    - Galatians 2:20, "I have been crucified with Christ and I no longer live, but Christ lives in me."

- "I was Saul, but you made me Paul"
  - Scripture Reference:
    - Acts 9:1–22—The story of Saul's transformation on the road to Damascus, where God changed his heart and mission.

- "All my sins have been nailed to the cross"
  - Scripture Reference:
    - Colossians 2:14, "Having canceled the charge of our legal indebtedness, …He has taken it away, nailing it to the cross."

- "I believe you set me free"
  - Scripture Reference:
    - John 8:36, "So if the Son sets you free, you will be free indeed."

- "Because I gave a bended knee"
  - Scripture Reference:
    - Philippians 2:10, "That at the name of Jesus every knee should bow."

- "Turn away from independence"
  - Scripture Reference:
    - Proverbs 3:5, "Trust in the Lord with all your heart and lean not on your own understanding."

- "Search forgiveness and repentance"
  - Scripture Reference:
    - Acts 3:19, "Repent, then, and turn to God, so that your sins may be wiped out."

- "Judgment is imminent"
  - Scripture Reference:
    - 2 Corinthians 5:10, "For we must all appear before the judgment seat of Christ."

- "His grace is mercy, water when you're thirsty"
  - Scripture Reference:
    - John 4:14, "But whoever drinks the water I give them will never thirst."

- "Stop being worldly"
  - Scripture Reference:
    - Romans 12:2, "Do not conform to the pattern of this world, but be transformed by the renewing of your mind."

My Feet Are Planted

[Chorus]
My feet are firmly planted now (yeah)
My feet are firmly planted now (yeah)
Deeply rooted in the ground
I was lost now I'm found
Make way I'm heaven bound
(Repeat)

I know a Creator even greater than Picasso

Modern Psalms, Volume 1

Who's known for saving lost souls
And doing the impossible
Repairs the broken back to whole
Served a sacrificial role
Now you got me on the roll
So let's go down this rabbit hole

Without Jesus we search pleasure and possession
Leading to possession and never seeing heaven
If you only seek desires
And the ones that you admire
It brings a new meaning
To getting fired with no severance
Wow

Place your faith in God above (yeah, yeah)
Witness what he's promised us (yeah, yeah)
His presence is obvious
Trade euphoria for true love

[Chorus]

Let your Holy Father take you fishing
He paid your admission
Through His crucifixion
Make him your physician
Take His prescription
Freedom from religion
Fact over fiction
You have to live grace

Not just make it a theology
It isn't a philosophy
Apply to be a prodigy
With honesty comes harmony
Peace from animosity
Eternity that's guaranteed
If you bend a knee so God can see
Do it

You're your own worst enemy
Get out of the way let Jesus teach
Submission to serenity
That's why He's called the Prince of Peace

[Chorus]

You don't make time for Jesus
You make Jesus your life
There is no compromise
In the pursuit of paradise
Want a love that satisfies
And a heavenly afterlife
Acknowledge Him and His sacrifice
Be careful who you idolize

You give hope to the hopeless
A voice to the voiceless
Help me to stay focused
And make the right choices
Free me of my disbelief
You're the only one I seek
Spirit's willing but the body is weak
So, strengthen every heartbeat

Let me only speak the truth (yeah)
Produce in me good fruit (yeah)
Protect and give me refuge
I can only love myself while trusting You

[Chorus]

Behind the Song

IN "MY FEET ARE PLANTED," THERE'S a beautiful interplay between the music and the message. The moment I heard the instrumental track from Piero DiGilio, it immediately set the tone for what I envisioned: a feel-good, yet thought-provoking song. The instrumental captured the emotional balance I was aiming for—something that lifts the spirit but also challenges the listener to reflect deeply about their spiritual journey. At the time, I wanted to write a song that was not only fun to listen to but also maintained spiritual integrity, sparking meaningful and theologically rich discussions.

One of the key metaphors I wanted to weave into this song is the idea of being deeply rooted in faith. This concept is prominent throughout the Bible. In both the Old and New Testaments, trees, plants, and roots often symbolize strength, growth, and a connection to God. Jesus Himself uses agricultural imagery in His parables, describing how faith grows, how the Kingdom of God flourishes, and how believers must remain rooted in Him to bear fruit.

For example, Psalm 1:3 describes a person of faith as "a tree planted by streams of water, which yields its fruit in season and whose leaf does not wither—whatever they do prospers." This image of a tree with deep roots, firmly planted by a life-giving source, is what I wanted to convey in the song. Being rooted in faith means being connected to Christ, drawing nourishment from Him, and being unshaken by the storms of life.

Similarly, in John 15:5, Jesus says, "I am the vine; you are the branches. If you remain in me and I in you, you will bear much fruit; apart from me, you can do nothing." This teaching resonates deeply with the message of my song: our spiritual life and growth depend entirely on our connection to Christ. Without that foundation, we are like plants with shallow roots, easily uprooted by the trials and storms of life.

The phrase "My feet are firmly planted" is a powerful declaration of faith that signifies spiritual maturity and a steadfast relationship with Christ. Like a tree with deep roots, I am anchored in my faith, drawing strength and nourishment from my connection with God. This deep-rooted faith provides stability, allowing me to stand firm even in the face of life's storms and trials.

Being deeply rooted also reflects spiritual growth—a process that doesn't happen overnight. It requires time, effort, and dedication to cultivate a mature faith. Through prayer, study of God's Word, and an ongoing relationship with Jesus, I've nurtured a faith that can withstand difficulties and uncertainties. The stronger the roots, the more unshakable the faith.

Ultimately, this declaration isn't just about resilience; it's about trust. By being deeply rooted, I express complete trust in Christ's power and promises. No matter how fierce the storm may be, I know that my relationship with Him will carry me through, and I will remain steadfast. The stability of this foundation empowers me to grow in faith, bear spiritual fruit, and stand firm in my calling as a follower of Christ.

In my lyrics, I use metaphoric language to express the glory of Christ, as in the line, "I know a Creator even greater than Picasso." This comparison emphasizes that our Divine Creator surpasses any masterpiece humanity could ever produce. While renowned artists like Picasso are celebrated for their talent and creativity, their works are mere shadows compared to the infinite beauty, intricacy, and majesty found in God's creation.

Everywhere we look, we can see the fingerprints of God. From the towering majesty of mountain ranges to the serene expanse of the seas, from the awe-inspiring diversity of wildlife to the simple, pure joy found in a baby's smile, all of creation reflects the glory of its Creator. Each detail testifies to His craftsmanship, and together, they reveal a greatness far greater than any human imagination could ever conceive.

Without the spiritual foundation of Christ, we are destined to fall into self-gratification, constantly seeking pleasures of the flesh. This doesn't necessarily mean pursuing inherently evil things, but even the "good" we do, without Christ, can be rooted in the false religion of "Self." In today's world, this is often seen in the way many people approach charity. Take,

In the Beginning

for example, social media influencers who record themselves performing acts of kindness, such as giving money or food to the homeless, but do so with a camera constantly rolling, showcasing their good deeds to the world for public praise. Their actions may appear compassionate, but without Christ at the center, the motivation often shifts from genuine love to self-promotion.

Jesus addresses this kind of self-serving behavior in Matthew 6:3, saying, "Do not let your right hand know what your left hand is doing." This verse is a crucial reminder to examine the motives behind our actions. Are we doing them for the praise of men, or to honor God? Are our good works carried out for the fleeting satisfaction of appearing righteous and gaining attention, or are they done out of genuine love and devotion to the King we claim to follow and serve?

One of the most sobering passages in Scripture comes from Matthew 7:21-23, where Jesus warns, "Not everyone who says to me 'Lord, Lord,' will enter the Kingdom of Heaven, but only the one who does the will of my Father who is in heaven." He goes on to describe how many will plead their case—declaring that they performed miracles and cast out demons in His name—yet He will respond, "I never knew you. Away from Me, you evildoers." These words serve as a powerful wake-up call urging us to examine whether our good works are truly done for God's glory, or for our own gratification. If they are done to boost our own ego or reputation, then we risk standing before God one day and hearing those terrifying words: "I never knew you. Away from Me."

I once heard a preacher explain that God made us from dirt for a reason. Dirt is humble—it's stepped on, it's lowly, and most people don't see much value in it. While many of us might prefer to think that we were made from gold or diamonds, the truth is, you can plant a seed in dirt, and from it springs life and transformation. Gold and diamonds can't nurture growth; their worth comes only from the value people assign to them. Dirt, on the other hand, becomes the foundation for something far greater—new life.

In the same way, a heart that's humble and open before God can bring forth life and transformation through Christ. When we allow Him to plant His Word within us, our faith takes root and begins to grow. Like good soil that receives both sun and rain, our hearts—though formed from something simple and lowly—become the very ground where His Spirit cultivates strength, fruitfulness, and deep spiritual roots.

I conclude the first verse with the phrase "trade euphoria for true love." This concept has been a recurring theme in earlier songs, but is one worth emphasizing. The world may offer us euphoria—those fleeting moments of joy and pleasure that are often so enticing—but such feelings are ultimately temporary and can leave us feeling empty once the moment passes. In contrast, our salvation in Christ introduces us to a profound, unconditional love—one that transcends anything the world has to offer.

This love is not just a passing emotion; it's a deep and abiding connection that cannot be replicated or found in any other source. It transforms our hearts and renews our minds, grounding us in a way that superficial feelings never could. Through this true love, we find lasting fulfillment and a deep sense of belonging that surpasses the temporary highs of earthly pleasures.

In the second verse, I begin with the invitation to "let your Holy Father take you fishing." This imagery serves as a powerful metaphor for the multifaceted nature of Jesus. He embodies both the nurturing qualities of a father and the moral guidance we seek, while also being a leader who exemplifies what it means to worship with authenticity and devotion.

One of the challenges we face in our faith journey is the presence of denominations and doctrines that often impose rules that go beyond the teachings of Scripture. These interpretations can sometimes become legalistic, constraining the freedom we have in Christ. When we break free from the chains of rigid doctrines and denominational boundaries, we uncover a sense of true freedom and joy in our walk with Christ.

This message is not a call to abandon your church or denomination; rather, it's an encouragement to remember that no church is perfect. The objective should be to find a community where you feel spiritually at home because ultimately, *you* are the Church. The physical building simply serves as a gathering place for fellowship with other believers. The Bible instructs us not to neglect this vital aspect of our faith.

I urge individuals to engage personally with Scripture and allow the Holy Spirit to guide their understanding. Teaching the Word should begin within our homes, while the pastor's role is to nurture the church community, offer support during struggles, and clarify the parts of Scripture that may be difficult to grasp.

It's essential to embody grace in our daily lives rather than merely viewing it as a theological concept. As we dedicate time throughout the week to study the Scriptures and gather for worship and fellowship on the seventh day, God's Word begins to take root in our hearts, transforming our understanding and deepening our relationship with Him.

When it comes to faith, we often find that we are our own worst enemies, consistently sabotaging ourselves in ways that undermine our spiritual journey. This self-sabotage stems from our inherent flaws and weaknesses as human beings. However, through our submission to Christ, we can discover serenity and strength that comes from His guidance, allowing His peace to quiet the turmoil within us.

In this submission, we are invited into a transformative experience— one that grants us a new life characterized by inner peace and fulfillment. Jesus is rightly referred to as the Prince of Peace because He provides the comfort and tranquility that our restless hearts seek. In Him, we find not only refuge from our struggles but also the path to healing and wholeness. Through His teachings and example, we learn to navigate life's complexities with grace and assurance, finding freedom from the inner turmoil that so often stems from our flawed human nature.

The third verse of this song opens with the powerful statement, "You don't make time for Jesus; you make Jesus your life." This highlights a crucial truth: too often, we place Jesus in the background of our lives, relegating Him to a secondary role. In reality, He is meant to be our focal point, the central figure around whom our lives revolve. To truly live in alignment with our faith, we must rearrange our priorities so that Christ remains at the forefront of our hearts and minds.

I want to emphasize that whenever I use the word "we" in this book, I am including myself in this reflection. I, too, have fallen into the trap of placing my own needs and desires above Christ. However, as I grow closer to Him, I find it increasingly easier to keep Him as my priority.

I often think about how people dedicate their entire lives to building a career, investing countless hours of hard work and sacrifice. Yet, at the end of that journey, when retirement comes, the company often moves on as if that employee never existed. The stark reality is that it is the family and friends who truly love and care for us who will mourn our passing, not the faceless entity of a corporation.

Given that our time on this earth is limited, it is essential to ensure that we are prioritizing the right things. We must focus on what truly matters—our relationship with Christ, our loved ones, and our spiritual growth—so that we can live lives of purpose and meaning.

If you ever find yourself feeling lost or disconnected from Christ, remember that it's perfectly okay to acknowledge those feelings and reach out to Him through prayer for help. The Lord delights in our willingness to turn to Him, especially in moments of weakness and uncertainty. If you're unsure how to express your thoughts or concerns in prayer, don't hesitate to seek guidance from your church elders or those who are seasoned in their faith. They can offer support, pray for you, and teach you how to articulate your struggles before God. In your prayers, be specific. Pray against intrusive thoughts that cloud your mind; pray against disbelief that shakes your faith. Seek strength, wisdom, and guidance to navigate your challenges. Jesus exemplified this vulnerability in the Garden of Gethsemane, where He openly admitted His need for the Father. Aware of the immense burden He was about to bear—the weight of humanity's sin and the suffering of the cross—Jesus prayed for God to take the cup away from Him. Yet, in perfect obedience, He surrendered to the Father's will, saying, "Not My will, but Yours be done."

Allowing yourself to feel vulnerable while praying is a beautiful expression of trust in our loving heavenly Father. It's essential to remember that God is not only present during the good times but also walks with us through our struggles and hardships. Embrace the comfort of His presence, knowing that He cares for you deeply—through both your triumphs and your trials.

> *"I want to preach it because I'm not ashamed of the good news.*
> *It is God's power to save everyone who believes."*
> —Romans 1:16 (paraphrased)

About PCM Music

PCM (Praise Christ Ministry) is not just a name; it is a testament to the transformative power of faith and music. As a devoted Christian music artist, PCM wears many hats, faithfully embracing the roles of husband and father alongside his musical calling.

In August 2023, PCM experienced a divine intervention when God placed a chorus in his mind—a melody that simply would not leave. Despite having no prior interest in pursuing music, he found himself continually drawn back to it. The melody lingered until September, when he finally put pen to paper and gave birth to the song "I No Longer Live." That moment marked the beginning of PCM's musical journey.

By October, "I No Longer Live" was recorded, igniting a deep and undeniable passion within him. From that point forward, PCM became a willing vessel for the Holy Spirit's message through music, his creativity now fueled by purpose rather than ambition. Since then, he has released an impressive collection of songs and collaborated with artists from around the world, including Missouri, Washington, Nigeria, Australia, and Russia.

Yet beyond the reach, recognition, and global collaborations, PCM remains firmly grounded in a single mission: to sow seeds of faith through music. With every lyric and every melody, he seeks to stir hearts, awaken spirits, and guide others toward a deeper relationship with Christ. PCM's story stands as a living testimony to the power of faith, music, and divine inspiration—a journey shaped by obedience, humility, and an unwavering commitment to sharing the message of love and redemption.

Most of PCM's music is made possible through donations. If you feel led to support this ministry, the information to do so is provided below.

Thank you, and God bless.

PCM

pcmmusic.com
pcmmusic4u@gmail.com

About Piero DiGilio

*** Note from Author: Piero DiGilio is the Exclusive Producer for PCM Music, but he's way more than just a producer to me. He's been there since my very first song, before I knew what I was doing or where any of this would go. He believed in the vision God gave me and supported me through every step, every mistake, every win, and every moment in between.

What started as just working together has turned into a real friendship. We've grown close over the years, and we share the same mission: using music to spread the Gospel and point people to Christ. Piero creates all of my instrumentals and handles the mixing and mastering too. Every track people hear from PCM Music has his fingerprints on it.

Honestly, PCM Music wouldn't be what it is today without him. I'm grateful God put him in my path.

PIERO DIGILIO WAS BORN IN ITALY in 1987. At the age of five, his family relocated to Germany, but after just a year, his parents separated and his father moved back to Italy. As the oldest of three children, Piero had to shoulder responsibilities early since his mother worked hard to support the family. Though their circumstances were modest, Piero notes that many had it worse, and they simply made do with what they had. With just a soccer ball and a few action figures, he developed a creative mind—one that later fueled his passion for writing stories.

By the age of twelve, Piero had already started writing rap lyrics and composing his first melodies. By twenty, he had gained local recognition with his group, Amageddo, a name blending *Armageddon* and *Ghetto* to symbolize "from nothing to the end." As the group's leader and motivator, Piero guided the collective through music production in their own studio. However, as time went on, some members became involved in crime and drugs, and Piero found himself increasingly disconnected from the street mentality that had defined their early years. He made the decision to part ways with the group and shifted his focus toward building a stable career with hopes of starting a family.

At twenty-four, Piero began producing beats on his own and discovered that he enjoyed being behind the scenes, away from the spotlight. Three years later, his first son was born, and he and his wife were married soon after. Their second son arrived just a year later. Now, at thirty-six, Piero continues to make music—often joined by his children, who are now seven and nine. Together, they enjoy creating music as a family, each one playing different instruments and sharing their creations. These moments of musical collaboration are what Piero cherishes most. He hopes that, as they grow, his children will also turn to music as a source of strength, creativity, and refuge from the negative influences of life.

Raised in a strict religious household, Piero believes that his upbringing shielded him from vices such as drugs and alcohol during his youth. The teachings he grew up with left a lasting impression, and even as an adult, he has no desire for substances that take away a person's self-control. Over the years, however, his perspective on religion began to shift. As a child, he often wondered why there were so many religions and questioned whether following the wrong one could lead to eternal damnation. His views began to evolve as he grew older, especially after witnessing scandals within religious institutions and becoming aware of what he perceived as dark influences, including those tied to the Jesuits within the Vatican.

Today, Piero holds firmly to the Ten Commandments, believing they form the moral foundation shared by many religions and provide a path to peace when lived out. His focus rests on the values they uphold rather than any specific religious institution. He continues to share his music with the world, offering his beats through platforms such as TikTok, Instagram, and Facebook under the handle "Gilio Beats."

KINGDOM BRIDGES
PUBLISHING

 Check out our projects at: kingdombn.com/publishing

 Find us on Socials @Kingdombn

 Find us on Streaming @Kingdombn

www.ingramcontent.com/pod-product-compliance
Lightning Source LLC
Chambersburg PA
CBHW050518100526
44581CB00001B/18